MW00569111

Stupidomics

Stupidomics

A Primer on the U.S. Economy

*How Economic Folly Broke It - How Economic
Wisdom Can Fix It*

William Hahn
and
Lyle Bowlin

NorthAmerican
Business Press

Miami – Toronto

North American Business Press, Inc
Miami, Florida 33064
Toronto, Canada
isbn: 978-0-615-29297-7
© 2009 All Rights Reserved.

Cover art by Jason Thomas.

Along with trade books for various business disciplines, the North American Business Press also publishes a variety of academic-peer reviewed journals.

Library of Congress Control Number 2009927480

Library of Congress
Cataloging in Publication Division
101 Independence Ave., SE
Washington, DC 20540-4320

Printed in the United States of America
First Edition
978-0-615-29297-2

Table of Contents

1. The Basics: Understanding Gross   17
   Domestic Product
2. Explaining the Economic Crisis   39
   of 2008
3. Understanding Fiscal and Monetary   51
   Policy Tools
4. How an Economy Can Grow Forever   59
5. The Rationale for Lowering Tax Rates   65
6. International Trade   69
7. Eliminating Stupidomics and Reducing   77
   the Risk of Economic Failure
8. Sacrifice and Changing Expectations   91
9. Final Word   95
   Glossary and Amplifications   97
   Test of Economic Understanding   105

Stupidomics

At the end of 2008, government leaders and most professional economists were looking at each other and asking, "How did we miss this?" and "Why didn't we see it coming?"

Indeed, why didn't they? Our answer to their question is— *Stupidomics*. Those asking these questions aided and abetted those who drove our economy to the brink of disaster. Words like hubris, myopia, folly, egoism, and pridefulness come to mind when we think about these noble custodians of America's economic wellbeing.

While our august leaders were blind to impending economic danger, we saw it coming. To be honest, we weren't sure when the economy would crash, and we didn't know how far it would fall. But, by using the simple circular flow concepts presented in this book, we were confident that a significant adjustment couldn't be avoided. Because of this conviction, in 2007 we made adjustments that protected our financial assets.

What we present in this book isn't rocket science. We simply cover basic economic principles in a way that can be understood by non-macroeconomics minded Americans. But our message is important, and the concepts we explore work.

Understanding fundamental economic concepts is essential, because economic decisions are imbedded in our jobs, how we spend our money, how our government spends our money, and how international trade impacts our nation. Indeed, economics is a primary decision factor when we vote in local and national elections. No matter how much we try, we can't escape the basic laws of economics—they are a daily fact of life.

Yet, as a country, we do a poor job of teaching the U.S. economic system to our citizens. In a 2005 study, The National Center for Economic Education found that only 15 states require that economics be taught in our public schools. In a country that lays claim to the world's largest economy and prides itself on its ability to create jobs, we find it peculiar that only 30 percent of Americans receive formal training on how our economy works.

We think that politics is mostly about economics. How can an electorate make informed decisions on candidates, and evaluate policy initiatives, if they do not understand basic economic concepts? The fact of the matter is, they can't.

Most Americans have an intuitive feel for how their lives are impacted by the ebb and flow of economic activity as the U.S. economy goes through an economic cycle. This sense of economic conduct is based on common sense. Interestingly, this sense is often correct. However, Americans lack depth of understanding when it comes to economic ideas advanced by the government. Their grasp of economic principles underlying policy initiatives would be fortified by formal training.

Such training should include lessons about how the U.S. economy in managed, how GDP is generated, how unemployment is defined, and how inflation is calculated. Those who are economically unschooled cannot possibly make informed decisions about candidates and issues.

To be sure, most Americans do not understand how the basic fiscal policy tools of taxing and spending impact economic growth. Even more elusive is their understanding of how the economy is affected by the Federal Reserve System (hereafter, "the Fed") through its conduct of monetary policy.

Those elected to the presidency and both houses of congress must deliberate about, and vote on, the Federal budget and international trade agreements. They must also decide whether to regulate or deregulate selected industries. Legislators vote on numerous issues that impact our local, state, and national economies. And yet, we suspect that most could not pass an undergraduate Macroeconomics 101 exam.

How does your economic knowledge measure up? Here's how you can find out. The National Council on Economic Education provides an opportunity to gauge your economic prowess. They provide a 20-question test that covers key economic concepts. This test can be taken by going to: http://www.ncee.net/cel/test/. It is immediately graded once you finish the exam. While the test does not cover all of the concepts included in an economics textbook, it does provide a way to find out where your understanding of economics ranks in term of others who have taken this exam.

We have provided a similar exam at the end of this book. We recommend you take it now. Then, once you have completed this book, retake it in order to determine how your economic knowledge has grown.

We think that passing an economics course should be a requirement of graduation from high school. We also understand that teaching economics to every high school student has a cost. But, not doing so is more costly. Former Harvard University president Derek Bok is quoted as saying, "If you think education is expensive, try ignorance." Every economic failure, whether it is an individual family or the U.S. economy as a whole, that could have been prevented had there been a better understanding of economic principles amplifies the cost of not training U.S. citizens in this area. The economic collapse of 2008 provides clear and compelling evidence of the cost of failing to educate citizens about macroeconomic principles.

It is this lack of economic understanding that motivated the title of our book--*Stupidomics*. The title is not meant to imply that Americans are stupid. Rather, we mean that Americans are not well schooled in the basic tenants of our economic system. As we see things, *Stupidomics* was a contributing cause of the financial institution crisis of 2008.

But the 2008 financial institution crisis is not the first one in U.S. economic history. It is, however, the first one to take place in the 21st Century. In recent times, the U.S. economy experienced a savings and loan crisis in the 1980s which resulted in over 700 failed institutions and cost U.S. taxpayers about $125 billion ($240 billion in current dollars).

In addition, there was a financial institution crisis in the early 1990's. Indeed, the FDIC reports that between 1980 and 1994, a total of 1,617 banks failed. These banks had assets totaling over $206 billion. Remarkably, this was a larger number of bank failures than occurred during the Great Depression. A study by the FDIC found that a wave of bank failures is always preceded by rapid GDP growth and rampant speculative investment activity. In this environment, real estate bubbles form—and eventually burst. Sound familiar from an October 2008 perspective? A wave of financial institution failures is always followed by a recession.

The repeated trouble within the financial institution industry is a perfect example of what Bok is referring to. The inability to learn from prior mistakes is an aspect of *Stupidomics*. The unresolved economic sins of the past contributed to the 2008 financial institution crisis and its mind numbing price tag of $700 billion and counting.

Philosopher George Santayana said, "Those who cannot remember the past are condemned to repeat it." In the economic sector, we are making Santayana look like he knew what he was talking about. Since the mid-1970's, the financial institution industry has been in crisis about every 10 years. The only way to prevent the upcoming $2-to-$3 trillion financial institution crisis of 2020 is to insure that all Americans understand basic economic principles.

In this book, we are not seeking to explain all of the theoretical concepts presented in a macroeconomics textbook. Some are too quantitative and others are too arcane to be useful to an understanding of fundamental economic principles. Rather, we seek to present a few basic concepts that will help readers understand how the U.S. economy grows, how sacrifice today can create a more robust economy for our children and grandchildren, and why further tax decreases, while tempting, are unwise. Our book also shows how the U.S. economy got so far out of balance that we are experiencing what most economists are calling the worst financial crisis since the Great Depression.

By presenting economics in a more readable manner, we are confident that Americans will benefit from our message. We hope so, for the more Americans know about the principles that underlie our economic system; the more likely it is that *Stupidomics* will be eliminated from both personal and governmental decisions.

About the Authors

William Hahn, DBA, CPA, is a Professor of Accounting at Southeastern University in Lakeland, FL. He is a CPA with professional experience at Ernst & Ernst (now Ernst & Young) and is a former banker (20 years) where he served as Chief Financial and Chief Operating Officer for publicly traded banking organizations. He has published professional and academic articles in the *ABA Banking Journal*, *The Ohio Banker*, *Bankers Magazine*, the *Journal of Business and Economic Studies*, the *Academy of Strategic Management Journal*, the *Journal of Education for Business*, *Accounting Forum*, and the *International Journal of Bank Marketing*.

Lyle Bowlin, DBA, is the Vice President of Academic Affairs at Southeastern University in Lakeland, FL. His educational background includes extensive training in both economics and finance, subjects he has taught at both the University of Northern Iowa and Southeastern University for a combined total of 22 years. In addition, he served as the director of a Small Business Development Center for seven years. Dr. Bowlin has hosted a weekly radio show and published in the *Journal of Portfolio Management, Journal of Economics, Journal of Applied Management and Entrepreneurship, and the Journal of Education for Business.*

For our wives, Laura and Linda.

And a special thanks to those who reviewed our manuscript and whose comments helped to improve our work. Thank you Samantha Audette, Lauren Burris, and Andrew Sherbo.

1

The Basics: Understanding Gross Domestic Product

Gross Domestic Product ("GDP") is the measure used to monitor U.S. economic growth. GDP is defined as the market value (i.e., selling price) of all goods and services produced within the U.S.'s border during one year.

To understand GDP, the circular flow concept is a useful learning tool, as this model provides a way to conceptualize how our economy works. Obviously, the U.S. economy is much more complicated than our presentation suggests. But, to try to teach everything that is happening in our economy all at once would be to teach nothing.

Thus, to provide useful economic insight, we will keep our discussion at a basic level. We are hopeful that this will not only prove educational, but will also inspire many to pursue further education in this area.

We start with a simple circular flow concept and then add saving, government, and international activities in order to illustrate how these areas impact economic growth. We are confident that by the time you get to the end of this book, you will experience an "economic eureka."

Simple Circular Flow

The simple circular flow concept assumes that an economy is made up of households and businesses. For discussion purposes, we will first look at circular flow from the viewpoint of an individual family. Then we will discuss the economy as a whole.

The circular flow idea for an individual family is illustrated in Figure 1. In this illustration, our family (household in economic language) supplies labor to a business. In return for the family's labor, the business pays our family a wage. This exchange is illustrated by the bottom loop in the figure.

In this example, we assume that all money earned by our family is spent on goods and services. To accomplish this, our family buys goods and services (groceries, cars, etc.) and in return they use the money earned from wages to pay for these purchases. This spending on goods and services represents GDP and is illustrated by the upper loop in circular flow diagram shown in Figure 1.

The basic idea is that money continuously flows from business to family and back to business as labor/wage and purchase/payment transactions occur throughout the year.

Figure 1
Circular Flow For Consumer Spending: Single Family

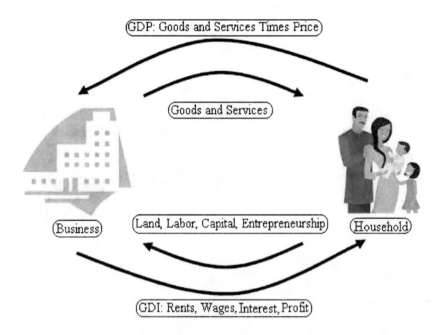

Also, in our example, we assume that our family does not save; that there is no government, and therefore, no taxes to pay; and that an international market does not exist. We do this to simplify the discussion of the circular flow concept. These additional market realities are added through the remainder of this chapter.

While our introduction to the circular flow concept focuses on an individual family and one business, the U.S. Census Bureau reports that in the U.S. economy there are approximately 105,480,000 households and 22,975,000 businesses.

Each household supplies a different set of resources to businesses. Some, as in our example above, supply labor. Others provide land, capital (i.e., households invest in or loan money to a business), and entrepreneurship (small business startups). Economists call these the factors of production. These transactions are shown in the bottom loop of the U.S. economic system flowchart shown in Figure 2.

Figure 2
Circular Flow For Consumer Spending: U.S. Economy

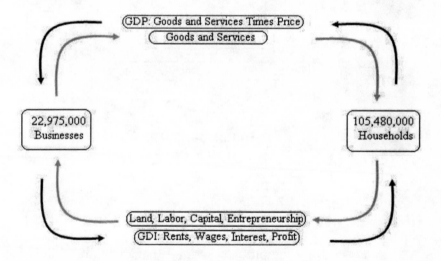

In return, all U.S. households receive payments based on the type of factor they provide to businesses. For labor, the payment is wages. For land, businesses pay rent. For investment capital, the payment is interest and dividends, and for entrepreneurship the business owners earn profits.

The sum of all payments received by households represents the total income earned in the U.S. for a year. Economists call this Gross Domestic Income (GDI).

As was the case with our single family illustration, we assume that U.S. households use ALL of their income to purchase goods and services from businesses. This exchange is represented by the upper loop in the circular flow diagram. And, since all goods that are produced by businesses are purchased by households, the upper loop represents GDP. In 2007, U.S. GDP amounted to about $13.8 trillion.

This relationship can be expressed as:

GDP = Consumer Spending.

Economists present this equation as:

$Y = C$, where Y stands for GDP and C stands for consumer spending.

Thus, in the simple circular flow, consumer spending makes up 100 percent of GDP. As a result, the simple GDP equation can be stated in percentage terms as:

GDP (Y) (100%) = C (100%).

Since all income is spent on goods and services, the lower loop must equal the upper loop. Therefore, GDP = GDI.

In 2007, GDP was about $13.8 trillion. Consumer spending makes up about 70 percent of this amount, or about $9.7 trillion. Government spending, investment, and international trade accounts made up the other $4.1 trillion. We will illustrate how investment, government, and international trade contribute to GDP in the following three sections.

Government Taxing and Spending

In reality, households don't spend all of their income. Some is taxed away by government for use in supplying public goods (e.g., roads, defense, & legal system). Taxes come in a variety of forms, with the most common being the income tax, social security tax, and property tax. This is added to the circular flow diagram for our single family as shown in Figure 3.

Figure 3
Circular Flow For Consumer Spending And Government Spending: Single Family

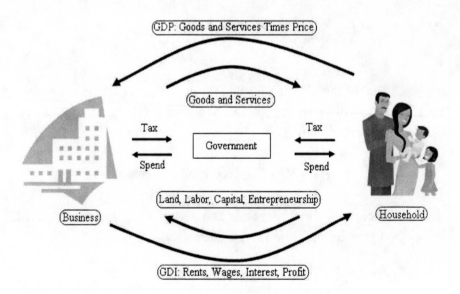

If our example family earns $100,000 per year, approximately $20,000 will be paid in Federal income tax and another $10,000 will be paid in social security, medicare, and similar taxes. These taxes reduce our family's gross income from $100,000 to disposable income of $70,000. Disposable income is normally deposited into a checking account and spent on goods and services.

What happens to the $30,000? It finds its way into the circular flow through government spending and through transfer payments to other households. The primary impact on the circular flow is that someone in the government, rather than the wage earner, gets to decide what gets purchased.

For the economy as a whole, the process works the same way as for the individual family, except that there are 105,480,000 households and 22,975,000 businesses paying taxes to, and receiving payments from, the government. This is shown in Figure 4.

Figure 4
Circular Flow For Consumer Spending And Government Spending: U.S. Economy

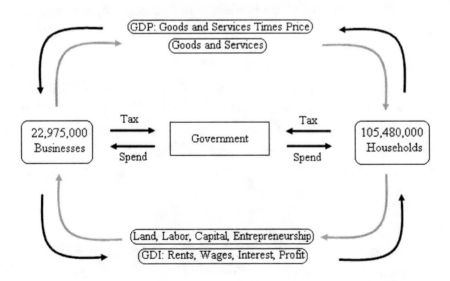

When government taxes households and spends all of the tax dollars it receives on public goods and services, the GDP equation is modified. Government is included in the GDP equation as "G".

The new expression is:

$$GDP = C + G.$$

If we assume that total tax collections in the economy are 20 percent of GDP (e.g. total tax paid by businesses and households divided by total GDP), then the GDP equation is expanded as follows:

$$GDP\ (100\%)\ =\ C\ (80\%) + G\ (20\%).$$

As indicated above, government spending is similar to consumer spending. The primary difference is that when dollars are taxed away from households, consumer choice is eliminated. Rather, the tax revenue received by the government is spent on goods and services, but the decision on what to buy is made by a government official. In 2007, total tax collections by the U.S. government amounted to just under $3 trillion.

The overall impact on total GDP is not changed when government tax dollars and related spending are equal. In other words, when every dollar that is taken away from households is spent by the U.S. government, total GDP does not change. In this case, there is no surplus or deficit and the government's budget is in balance.

The economy is, however, impacted when the government runs a budget surplus or deficit. A surplus occurs when tax collections exceed spending. Conversely, a deficit is realized when spending exceeds tax collections.

A budget surplus reduces GDP. To show how, we present an extreme example. If 20 percent of household income is taxed away from households, and none of it is spent by the government, household purchases would fall by 20 percent, and GDP would fall by the same 20 percent. This is because the tax reduces consumer spending by the amount paid to the government. If the government does not spend the amount received, goods and services are not purchased and total dollar GDP goes down.

A more typical example is when the government taxes away 20 percent of household income and spends only 19 percent on goods and services. In this case, the federal budget runs a surplus of one percent of GDP. Total dollar GDP will go down by the amount of the government surplus—or one percent of total GDP.

Conversely, if the government's total tax revenue is 20 percent of GDP, and the government spends more than 20 percent for goods and services, the government will experience a budget deficit. This is because the difference between the total tax revenue and total spending must be made up with borrowed money.

For purposes of illustration, let's assume that tax revenue is 20 percent of GDP. The government spends at a rate of 22 percent of GDP. Now the Federal budget is in deficit by two percent of GDP and the government borrows in order to fund its deficit. This will cause total GDP to rise by the amount of deficit spending (i.e., 2% of GDP). This in turn causes total dollar GDP to be higher than it would otherwise would have been had the budget been in a balance.

Taxing and spending are the fiscal policy tools employed by the U.S. government. These tools can be used to fine tune the economy as it goes through an economic cycle. Here's how. When the economy is strong, government should operate at a surplus in order to slow economic growth. On the other hand, when the economy is weak, the government should run a deficit in order to speed up economic growth. This is essentially how economic policy has been conducted for the past 60 years, and it is based on ideas set forth by British Economist John Maynard Keynes.

The goal in this section is to introduce how government activity impacts GDP. We will illustrate how Keynesian principles are employed by the U.S. government later in this chapter.

Saving and Investment

Another refinement of the circular flow concept is saving and investment. While the circular flow concept assumes that all income is spent on goods and services, this is not economic reality. Not all that is earned is spent. Saving and investment are added to the simple circular flow diagram for our individual family as shown in Figure 5. This activity is illustrated by deposits flowing into the banking system and loans being made by banks to both households and businesses.

For purposes of illustration, we assume that our family saves 21.4 percent of disposable income (i.e., total income minus taxes). Remember that this family earns $100,000 and pays taxes of $30,000. This family's disposable income is $70,000. Rather than spend the entire $70,000 on goods and services, our example family saves $15,000 (15 percent of GDP for illustration purposes) which they put into a bank in the form of a savings account or certificate of deposit.

Why does our family save? They save in order to build a fund of money that will allow them to buy big ticket items in the future, such as a house or car. They also save in order to pay for future college tuition for their children or to build a retirement fund. Or, they may simply save for "a rainy day" (i.e., a recession).

Once this money is in a bank, the bank then loans it to families who are buying a car, a home, or other consumer good. This is how saving by our family finds its way into the circular flow and contributes to economic growth.

Figure 5
Circular Flow For Consumer Spending, Government Spending, and Saving and Investment: Single Family

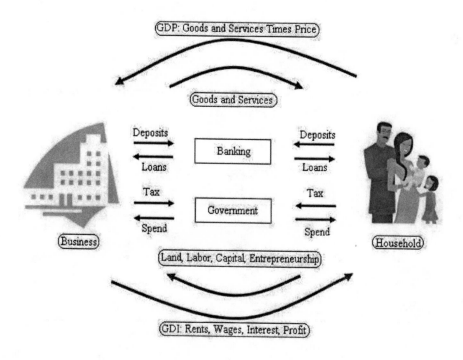

The same thing happens for the entire economy as shown in the circular flow diagram presented in Figure 6.

As discussed above, there are a variety of reasons that households and businesses do not spend all that they earn. Financial institutions gather these funds in the form of deposits (the economic term is saving). Amounts on deposit are then lent to households and businesses which, in turn, use the loan proceeds to buy new equipment, new buildings, or new homes. Loans (primarily credit card loans) are used to meet temporary cash shortfalls. When money saved is borrowed and used to purchase capital goods (e.g., buildings and machinery) the economic term is investment. The symbol for investment is "I" in the GDP equation.

When saving and related investment is added to the GDP equation, it expands to:

$$GDP = C + G + I.$$

Figure 6
Circular Flow For Consumer Spending, Government Spending, and Saving and Investment: U.S. Economy

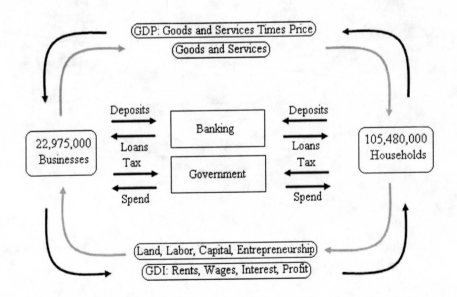

If we assume that saving, and related investment, in the U.S. economy is 15 percent of GDP, then the GDP equation is expressed as:

$$GDP\ (100\%) = C\ (65\%) + G\ (20\%) + I\ (15\%).$$

Notice that "C" goes down from 80 percent of GDP to 65 percent of GDP as a result of saving in the U.S. economy. GDP remains at 100 percent. This is possible because our presentation simplifies the banking process by assuming that ALL of the money that households save is loaned to both businesses and households. A further assumption is that these borrowers spend all the amounts borrowed on homes and other capital goods.

Saving and investment is an important economic function, because financial institutions provide an efficient mechanism for bringing depositors and borrowers together.

How so? If there were no financial institutions, households with excess earnings would have two choices. One is to keep unspent money hidden under a mattress or buried in the backyard. The other is to find someone in the community who wants to borrow money. When a borrower is found, a lending household would need to perform a credit analysis, make a loan, and collect loan payments. This is not efficient on a loan-by-loan basis. The banking system lowers individual transaction costs by making the saving and lending process more efficient through specialization and economies of scale.

Notice that when financial institutions loan 100 percent of deposits, circular flow equilibrium is restored since all money saved is spent by borrowers. It is generally assumed that borrowed money is primarily used to construct buildings, equipment, and other long-lived assets.

In reality, financial institutions cannot loan 100 percent of deposits. The U.S. banking system uses a fractional reserve approach which requires that about 10 percent of deposits be maintained "on reserve" with the Fed. Reserve funds cannot be loaned.

Also, for liquidity reasons, banks purchase investment securities (i.e., bonds and common stock). Reserves invested in bonds and stocks are not available to a bank for lending purposes. On average, the banking system loans about 70 percent of all amounts on deposit. As we will discuss later, reserve requirements are one of the three tools of monetary policy.

There is one additional aspect of the circular flow concept that we have not considered to this point. This is the multiplier effect related to government deficit spending and to the making of loans by the banking system. These multipliers allow GDP to grow at a faster rate than would otherwise be possible because of the manner in which funds circulate. This concept is more fully explored in the glossary.

Net Exports

The final component of the circular flow concept is net exports. This position is developed by subtracting imports from international markets from exports to international markets. The net export contribution to GDP is added to the circular flow diagram for our household as shown in Figure 7.

Our illustrative family can obtain goods from international markets in one of two ways. They can buy a product from a business that has imported it. Or, they can go directly to the international market and make a purchase. For example, oil companies import oil and then refine it into products consumed by households. On the other hand, our family might purchase a computer directly from a Japanese company.

Figure 7
Circular Flow For Consumer Spending, Government Spending, Saving and Investment, and Trade: Single Family

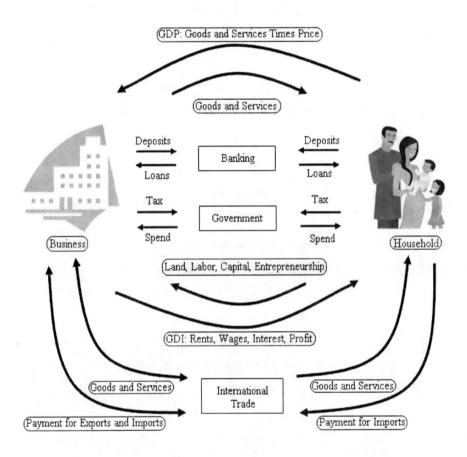

For the economy as a whole, the same concept applies as was presented for or illustrative family. The 105,480,000 households obtain most of their imported products through the business sector which conducts most of the importing and exporting activity in the U.S. economy. For example, consumers buy a variety of foreign products from the local Walmart store. These import transactions find their way into U.S. GDP as they flow from international sources to businesses to households. Payments flow back to international sources in the same manner as for that of the goods and services imported. This is illustrated in Figure 8.

The opposite happens with exports. Businesses make products which are sent to international markets. In return, dollars flow back from these markets to U.S. businesses.

Figure 8
Circular Flow For Consumer Spending, Government Spending, and Saving and Investment: U.S. Economy

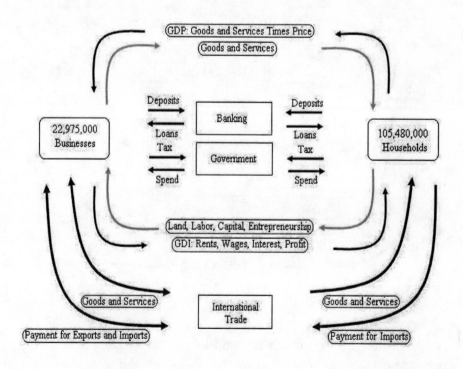

When the net export position (indicated with an "X" by economists in the GDP formula) is added to the GDP formula, it is expressed as:

$$GDP = C + G + I + X.$$

It is now time to rearrange the components of the GDP formula. For purposes of presenting the circular flow idea, we started with consumers, then added government, investment, and international trade. Economists normally show investment before government when discussing this formula. Therefore, from this point forward, we will present the formula as:

$$GDP = C + I + G + X$$

Currently, the net export position in the U.S. economy is minus five percent of GDP. This negative position is called a trade deficit. In others words, the U.S. imports more than it exports. The GDP equation, as fully expanded, is stated as:

$$GDP\ (100\%)\ =\ C\ (70\%) + I\ (15\%) + G\ (20\%) + X\ (-5\%).$$

As we discussed earlier, import and export transactions that impact GDP can be made by households, businesses, and/or government. This activity is messy and hard to explain. To simplify our example, we assume that net exports primarily impact consumers. Thus, to balance the GDP circular flow equation, consumer spending is increased from 65 percent as we left it after introducing governmental activity to 70 percent of GDP in the final equation presented above.

It is important to remember that exports and imports are substantial. In 2007, exports amounted to about $1.6 trillion. This was about 12 percent of total GDP. Imports amounted to $2.4 trillion, or about 17 percent of total GDP. The net export position was minus $700 billion. This is shown in the GDP equation above as minus five percent.

To provide perspective of the types of products included in the 2007 net export position, selected products imported and exported and their total dollar value are set forth in Table 1.

Table 1
Selected 2007 Import and Export Categories (In billions)

Product Type	Imports	Exports	Net Position
Computer & Electronic	$313	$137	$ 176 Imp
Transportation Equipment	278	202	76 Imp
Oil & Gas	229	10	219 Imp
Chemicals	160	147	13 Imp
Machinery, Except Electrical	121	123	2 Exp
Petroleum & Coal Products	102	31	71 Imp
Miscellaneous Mfg.	95	38	47 Imp
Electrical Equip., Appliances & Components	67	33	34 Imp
Fabricated Metal Products	50	30	20 Imp
Foods, Feeds, & Beverages	46	68	22 Exp

Source: Developed from data available at TradeStats Express

In dollar terms, the net U.S. trade deficit in 2007 was about $700 billion. As Table 1 shows, about 33 percent of the 2007 trade deficit resulted from oil and gas and other petroleum and coal products. Another 30 percent was caused by a net import position in autos and other transportation equipment. While there are a number of product areas where U.S. exports are greater than imports, the U.S. has a substantial trade advantage in foods, feeds, and beverages.

GDP and the Business Cycle

As the U.S. economy moves through a business cycle, the federal government and the Fed, each take actions aimed at preventing the economy from overheating during times of prosperity and from sinking too low during times of recession. A typical business cycle is illustrated in Figure 9.

Prior to the 1980s, the U.S. economy moved from prosperity to recession to prosperity every three to five years. Recently, the U.S. economy entered its 11th in the past 60 years in December 2007. Over the past 20 years, the cycle has lengthened to about ten years. Experts attribute the lengthening cycle to two factors. First, there has been a move from a manufacturing to a service-based economy. Second, there was a change in the manner that fiscal and monetary policy initiatives have been conducted over this timeframe.

Drawing on the work of John Maynard Keynes, economic textbooks teach that when the economy is prosperous, fiscal policy should manage the Federal budget into a surplus. Doing so slows GDP growth. Similarly, monetary policy should be conducted in a way that pushes interest rates up. These actions serve to reduce the rate of growth of the money supply. Slower money supply growth causes interest rates to rise. Higher interest rates reduce the demand for loans and, as a result, bank lending slows down.

Figure 9
Typical Business Cycle

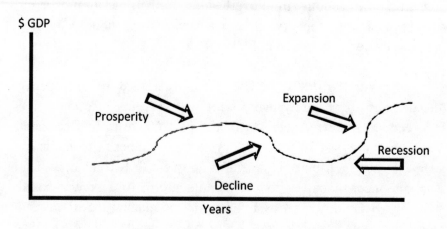

These fiscal and monetary policy actions work to slow the rate of growth of GDP. Failure to take these actions during times of prosperity allows the economy to overheat, which eventually results in inflation.

On the other hand, when the economy is in recession, policy makers should run a federal budget deficit and monetary policy should be conducted in a way that increases the money supply. This policy action pulls interest rates down which in turn encourages borrowing by households and businesses. Increased borrowing and spending by businesses and consumers promotes GDP growth.

While the Fed has generally done a credible job of managing monetary policy since 1980, the Federal government has generally failed to meet its fiscal policy obligations. How so?

Taxes have consistently been lowered since the 1980s. The lone exception is the Clinton tax increase in 1993. Conversely, not once during this period did U.S. government reduce total spending. Rather, they obfuscated the tax and spend issue by talking about slowing down the rate of spending growth. This is a common political red herring.

Consider this personal example. Assume your income has gone up by five percent per year for the past three years and that you have increased your consumption spending by the same five percent. This year, however, the economy is in recession and you do not get a pay raise. You increase your spending by only three percent this year. Your rate of spending has decreased from five percent to three percent, but, your total spending has still gone up. To make up the difference between no wage increase and the three percent spending increase, you will need to borrow money.

It works the same way with the Federal government. If the tax rate is reduced, the Federal government's income (tax revenue) falls. This is ok if total dollar spending is cut by the same amount. For example, if tax revenue falls by $100 billion and total government spending is cut by $100 billion, the budget stays in balance.

The problem is when taxes are cut by $100 billion and spending goes up by $200 billion (1.5% growth rate). Without the tax cut, spending might have gone up by $500 billion (3.8% growth rate). Thus, the rate of annual growth of spending goes down from 3.8 percent to 1.5 percent. But, and it is a big but, total dollar spending still goes up. This can only result in a budget deficit, which, in turn, contributes to an increase in the total U.S. debt level.

To offset a tax cut in a way that keeps the budget in balance, the Federal government should reduce spending by the same total dollar amount as tax revenue foregone.

Some argue that lowering income tax rates actually increases total tax revenue. This is partially true, but is misleading because existing tax rates have to be above 2008 levels before such a result can be realized. We address this more fully in a later chapter.

As was discussed above, when the government spends more that it receives from tax revenue, this results in a budget deficit that has an expansionary impact on the economy. The consistent use of budget deficits was a contributor to a financial extravagance of the past twenty-five years. This economic practice built an economic bubble that could not be sustained. The ultimate result was the remarkable collapse of the U.S. financial system in 2008.

Indeed, prior to 1972 the federal budget was in a slight surplus position, or close to it, year-after-year. However, since that time, the federal budget has been managed into a deficit position in every year except for the 1998 to 2001 timeframe. During this short time, the budget was in surplus primarily because of tax increases enacted in 1993.

So how can Americans use the circular flow and economic cycle idea to understand how the U.S. economy is being managed? We provide an illustrative example in the next chapter.

2

Explaining the Economic Crisis of 2008

In the previous chapter, we explained GDP by using the circular flow concept. To do this we used the GDP equation to explain how the U.S. economy operates: The equation is:

$$GDP\ (100\%)\ =\ C\ (70\%) + I\ (15\%) + G\ (20\%) + X\ (-5\%)$$

This equation can be used to determine where economic growth is being generated. It can also be used to evaluate whether GDP growth is built on a solid foundation or if it is built upon a bed of quicksand. Here's how.

Consumer Spending

Consumer spending is fundamentally sound when it is derived from earned income. However, the Economic Policy Institute points out that during the 2003 – 2007 timeframe real wages (the difference between actual wage increases and an increase in the rate of inflation) declined. This real decline was experienced by all wage earners except the very wealthy. In other words, for most Americans the annual growth rate of inflation exceeded the growth rate of household income. At the same time, real personal consumption grew at about a three percent annual rate.

How is this possible?

The answer is that consumers used credit card and second mortgage debt to supplement real wage shortfalls. This expansion of consumer debt served to increase consumer spending well above a level that made economic common sense.

Indeed, consumer borrowing lifted total household debt to an all time high. Figure 10 shows that consumer debt grew from about 58 percent of total GDP in 1990 to almost 100 percent of GDP by the end of 2007. The trend line in Figure 10 shows total household debt as a percentage of GDP using the 1990 level of 58%. We use this as a recent benchmark, not as a suggested desirable consumer debt level. It is easily seen that the consumer debt bubble started slowly in the late 1990's and then began to accelerate rapidly in 2001. The total 2007 consumer debt level amounts to about $120,000 per U.S. household.

Caution is warranted. Households can only take on so much debt. Sooner or later, they must reduce spending in order to pay debt down to manageable levels. Such personal financial management will be challenging since it appears that real wage growth will remain low into the foreseeable future.

Consumer spending will decline when consumers start to pay down their debt burden toward 1990 levels. This pay down of debt will result in slower GDP growth than might otherwise have been realized had the bubble never occurred.

Figure 10
Household Debt as a Percent of GDP

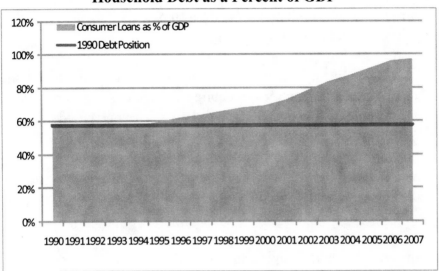

Source: Developed from Federal Reserve and Bureau of Economic Analysis data

Stupidomics: We estimate that during the 2003-2007 time period the bubble in consumer debt pushed GDP growth higher by two to four percentage points per year than would otherwise have been the case. This is an aspect of *Stupidomics*.

Politicians, of course, took credit for the GDP growth of the 2003-2007 timeframe. At the time, they claimed that solid, fundamental economic activity was the reason that the U.S. economy was growing at such a steady, prosperous rate. These politicians want Americans to believe it is their sage leadership and economic savvy that drives the U.S. economic engine.

Now you know better.

Investment

Investment is made possible by saving. During the 2003-2007 economic expansion, the average U.S. saving rate was about

1.5 percent of disposable income. This is low by historical standards. While saving was growing at this meager rate per year, investment was growing at about a seven percent rate, driven in part by the construction of new housing.

The housing boom was encouraged by financial institutions that abandoned the traditional requirement that home buyers make a 10 to 20 percent down payment when a home is purchased. In other words, prior to the current age of immediate gratification, a lender would only finance 80 to 90 percent of the purchase price of a home. The difference between the purchase price and the amount loaned is called owner's equity.

A down payment is important for three reasons. First, it requires that a home buyer learn to sacrifice in order to accumulate the amount needed to satisfy lending requirements. This is an important life skill that promotes personal financial responsibility. Second, it is economically advantageous for a homebuyer. A sizeable down payment reduces the amount borrowed which in turn reduces the monthly loan payment and also reduces the total interest paid to a financial institution over the life of a loan. Third, if a homeowner has equity in a home, he or she is less inclined to give up that equity by walking away from a home mortgage obligation when times get tough.

During the past five years, lenders veered away from time tested lending practices. Lured by herd mentality, lenders made loans at, or sometimes in excess of, the home's fair market value. In other words, if a home had an appraised market value of $100,000 these lenders would make a loan for $100,000 or more.

This, of course, all too often resulted in homes being purchase at a price that an owner could not afford. Indeed, financial institutions offered loan deals at levels well beyond what economic rationality would support.

The belief was that home prices would increase rapidly, and that these price increases would eventually bring the market value of a home above the amount of a loan's principal. Given sufficient time, a home's market value would rise to a point where a loan's principal amount would become 80 percent or less of the home's market value.

This is the type of thinking that spawns financial bubbles. The 2008 housing bubble is clearly seen in Figure 10, but, as is the case with all bubbles, this one burst. When it did, it contributed to the failure of Lehman Brothers, Fannie Mae, Freddie Mac and many other financial institutions in 2008.

Stupidomics: As a result of the U.S. housing bubble, GDP growth from 2003-2007 was higher than it otherwise would have been had traditional lending practices been followed. Both consumer spending ("C") and investment ("I") benefited from these excesses. We estimate that growth from housing investment inflated annual GDP growth statistics by one to two percentage points over where they would have been had historical lending standards been enforced.

As we pointed out in our discussion of consumer spending, politicians were quick to take credit for GDP growth between 2003 and 2007. They wanted Americans to know that it was their economic judiciousness that prospered the U.S. economy.

Now you know better.

Government

Government spending currently accounts for about 20 percent of GDP. This is up from the more common 18 percent when the budget is in balance. Thus, as the U.S. government borrowed to finance the war on terror, the invasion of Iraq, and the bailout of financial institutions; the budget deficit grew to unprecedented levels. A current estimate projects the 2008 deficit to approach $1 trillion.

A major contributor to the budget deficit was the Bush Administration's decision to fight the War in Iraq and the War on Terror without raising taxes to fund it. As Bank, Stark, and Thorndike point out in their book *War and Taxes*, the U.S. has a history of wartime fiscal prudence. They show that, while wartime presidents have been reluctant to raise taxes, they still did so for the economic health of the country.

Indeed, Bank et al. point out that wartime leaders were, "Unwilling to risk domestic achievements, or fearful of eroding support for an unpopular war, they [past presidents] have shrunk from the tough decisions that wars invariably demand. Eventually, however, they all accepted the hard realities. Whether ardent tribunes of fiscal sacrifice (like Franklin Roosevelt) or reluctant champions of fiscal responsibility (like Lyndon Johnson), they all accepted the need to some sort of home front sacrifice, as both an economic and moral necessity."

That is until the Bush Administration. This administration funded the Iraq war, the war on terror, the *Economic Stimulus Act of 2008*, and the *Emergency Economic Stabilization Act of 2008* with borrowed money. As a result, total Federal debt outstanding has grown to excess of 70 percent of GDP. It is likely to go higher when the financial institution bailout plan is fully implemented.

As the previous circular flow discussion highlighted, when a government spends more that it takes in from tax revenues, it must borrow the difference. Such borrowing has a positive, expansive impact on GDP. This is clearly shown in Figure 11. Indeed, since 1980, with a short respite during the Clinton administration, government policy has been to constantly increase the nation's total debt burden.

Stupidomics: The growth of government debt since 1980 positively impacted GDP growth from then to now. Remember, when a government borrows in order to spend, the economy grows at a faster rate than would otherwise be realized if the budget remains in balance.

We estimate that the increases in government deficit spending from 2003 to 2007 caused GDP growth to be overstated by one to three percentage points each year. Total U.S. government debt outstanding is currently somewhere around $11 trillion. This represents about $100,000 per U.S. household. If we add the $120,000 of consumer debt to the U.S. government amount, each household in the U.S. owes an average of $220,000. Wow!

Government leaders would have Americans believe that their actions in managing the U.S. budget were based on sound economic principles that were taken in the best interest of the nation's economy— both now, and for our children and grandchildren.

Now you know better.

Net Exports.

As a result of continuing budget shortfalls from 2003 to 2007, the U.S. dollar has fallen against most major currencies. This causes imports to be more expensive for U.S. consumers (which is inflationary) and exports to be less expensive in foreign markets (which increases the sales of U.S. goods and services). When exports increase relative to imports, GDP goes up. We estimate that the positive impact on U.S. GDP growth resulting from a weak dollar was between zero and one percent of total GDP

Figure 11
Total National Debt as a Percent of GDP

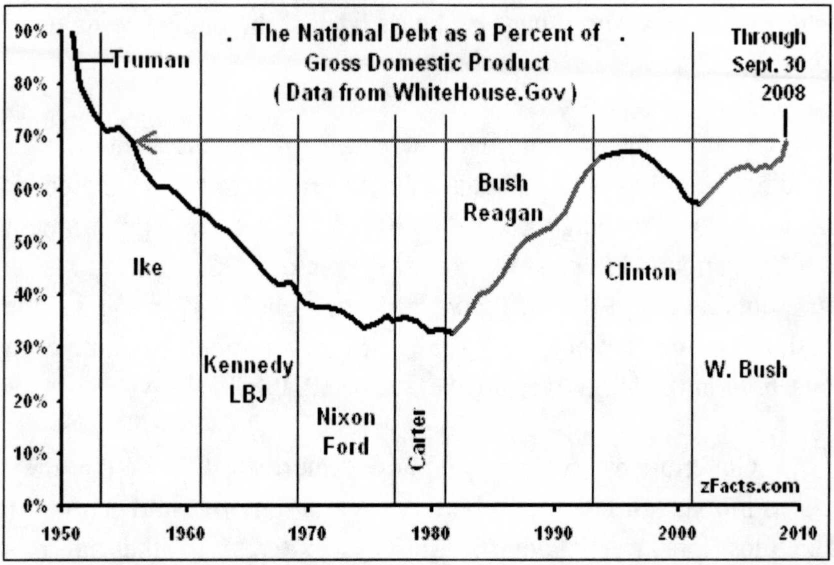

Source: http://zfacts.com/p/318.html. Adapted with permission.

Summing It Up

As we discussed above, from 2003 to 2007, there were several factors that made it appear that GDP was growing faster than solid economic fundamentals could support. In the remainder of this chapter, we use the GDP equation to illustrate why this is so. We also evaluate GDP growth with the bubble causing activity removed. This provides a view of what the GDP growth numbers might have looked like without the household and national debt extravagances previously discussed.

Our analysis suggests that during the four years from 2003 through 2007, each component of GDP included activity that is not normally present. These activities caused GDP growth to be overstated in each of these years.

Our analysis is summarized using the circular flow equation developed in earlier chapters. Specifically:

GDP (overstated by 4- 10%) = C (overstated by 2-4%) + I (overstated by 1-2%) + G (overstated by 1-3%) + X (overstated by 0-1%).

When these nonrecurring growth factors are used to adjust reported GDP, the normalized GDP growth is much less impressive as shown in Table 2.

Table 2
Normalized GDP Growth

Year	Reported GDP Growth	Removal 100% of *Stupidomics* Excess Growth	Removal 50% of *Stupidomics* Excess Growth	GDP Inflation Deflator	Inflation Adjusted 50% Excess Real GDP Growth
2004	6.8%	-3.5%	1.7%	2.9%	-1.2%
2005	6.4%	-3.1%	1.7%	3.3%	-1.6%
2006	6.1%	-1.7%	2.2%	3.2%	-1.0%
2007	4.2%	-1.6%	1.2%	2.7%	-1.5%

Source: U. S. Department of Commerce, Bureau of Economic Analysis

When all of the excess *Stupidomics* growth is removed from reported GDP for the years 2004 through 2007, the normalized U.S. economy is in decline. Indeed, there would have been a recession in each of the past five years (a.k.a. depression) had it not been for the extravagances in consumer spending (C), government spending (G), and housing (I).

It may be unfair to remove all of the excess *Stupidomics* growth in order to normalize the GDP data. Looked at in a more moderate way, when only half the excess *Stupidomics* growth is removed from each year's reported GDP, the normalized growth rate would have been sluggish—somewhere between one and two percent per year.

However, focusing on the 50-percent *Stupidomics* normalized growth rate is deceptive because it is in current (nominal) dollars. When inflation is considered, real GDP growth over this four-year period is negative. The real growth rate is calculated by deducting annual GDP growth at the 50-percent *Stupidomics* level from the GDP Inflation Deflator. Such normalized, real GDP growth is shown in the rightmost column in Table 2.

The primary components of GDP growing to excess at the same time resulted from what we now clearly see as household and governmental debt bubble that cannot be sustained. Interestingly, those engaging in these debt-based activities convinced themselves that they were smarter than their forebears and that their ability to borrow would be never ending. Such a mindset starts innocently enough, but at some point herd mentality takes over and people lose their common sense. Once this happens, financial markets rise to unsustainable levels.

In his book *A Random Walk Down Wall Street*, Burton Malkiel calls a market that has been elevated to unsustainable levels a "castle in the air." By 2008, the U.S. economy had become a castle in the air. Eventually, all bubbles burst and the castle comes a tumbling down. That is what happened to the U.S. economy in September and October of 2008.

As a result of the magnitude of economic excess in the first decade of the twenty-first century, we believe that it will take longer than normal, and longer than most policy makers expect, to return household and governmental debt to traditional levels. During this time, GDP will languish.

Stupidomics

3

Understanding Fiscal and Monetary Policy Tools

The concepts that we discussed in previous chapters are useful in evaluating not only the quality of economic growth, but also the nation's economic direction. To illustrate how the GDP formula can be used this way, we examine the business cycle in conjunction with the fiscal and monetary tools available to both the both Federal government and the Fed, respectively.

The Federal government has two fiscal policy tools. Taxing and spending. These tools can be used to fine tune the economy, but cannot be used to ensure a robust and sustained economy. Here's how it works.

Keynesian economic thought suggests that when the U.S. economy is riding high and prosperity is rampant, taxes should be raised and/or government spending curtailed. This creates a budget surplus. The tax dollars not spent by the government are used to pay down debt. Since government spending falls, this policy action slows the GDP growth rate.

When the economy is in recession, fiscal policy actions should be taken to lower tax rates and/or to increase government spending. Lowering tax rates decreases total tax revenue. In turn, households get to keep more of their earnings. They spend this tax windfall on goods and services, and consumer spending ("C" in the GDP equation) goes up. In turn, the government experiences lower total tax revenue and must borrow to fund its spending. Another alternative is for the government to leave tax rates unchanged and simply buy more goods and services while borrowing the money to pay for this increased spending. These actions increase "G" in the GDP equation.

Any combination of expansionary fiscal policy actions puts additional funds into the economic circular flow. As a result, economic activity picks up and GDP growth improves. The negative, which is too often forgotten, is that the national debt burden goes up and will need to be repaid in the future.

Figure 12
Fiscal Policy, Monetary Policy and GDP

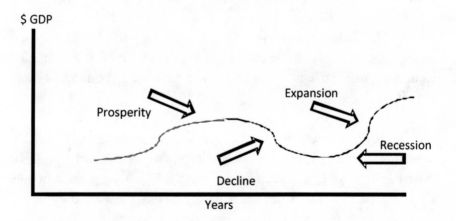

But fiscal policy has its limits. Taxes cannot be lowered too much and deficits can only get so large. Thus, fiscal policy managers must employ a combination of experience, courage, and instinct when making policy management decisions as the economy moves through an economic cycle.

At the end of 2008, the top marginal income tax rate was 35 percent. It is hard to see how this rate can be lowered in order to increase total tax revenue. Rather, tax cuts will lower total tax revenue, and any further reductions of tax revenue will increase an already burdensome total national debt position. We discuss this more fully in a later chapter.

Given the magnitude of total U.S. national debt, taxes should be raised in order to pay it down. But therein is the dilemma. Raising the tax rate is contrary to Keynesian thinking when an economy is in recession. And, continuing to increase the size of the deficit will result in future economic misery. Thus, because of fiscal imprudence in the past, which is an aspect of *Stupidomics*, policymakers are caught between the proverbial "rock and a hard place."

Monetary policy alternatives are equally bleak. The Fed has three tools that they use to manage the economy. These are reserve requirements, the discount rate, and open market operations.

Like fiscal policy, monetary policy cannot be used to control the economy. Monetary policy can only be used to fine tune it within a narrow range. Monetary policy can keep the economy from overheating during periods of prosperity and keep it from sinking too low during times of recession. The problem is that past monetary policy actions, that were taken out of economic necessity, and have subsequently been spiced with a dash of policy management imprudence, have left little room for the Fed to act as the economy slips into recession.

Here's why.

Reserve requirements are established by the Fed. For banks, reserve requirements set a limit on how much of each dollar on deposit at a bank can be loaned to businesses and individuals. Economists call this a fractional reserve system. Currently, reserve requirements on checking accounts are about 10 percent. This means that banks can loan $.90 for each dollar on deposit. The other $.10 must be maintained on reserve with the Fed for liquidity and safety reasons.

While the ability to adjust reserve requirements is the most powerful tool in the Fed's arsenal, it is seldom used. The last major adjustment was in 1990. That adjustment contributed to the economic prosperity of the 1990's.

The second tool available to the Fed is the discount rate, which is .5 percent near the end of 2008. This is the interest rate that the Fed charges member banks when they borrow money to meet short-term needs. Historically, this rate has averaged about 5.0 percent.

It is only possible to lower this rate to zero, which is a position where those who lend money get nothing in the way of a rate of return. If those with money cannot get a return for lending it, those with money are unlikely to lend it. Thus, there is little room for the Fed to maneuver with this policy tool.

As a practical matter, the discount rate is not an actively used monetary policy tool. Since the 1970s, this rate has been more of a following rate. The Fed tends use changes in the discount rate to confirm the direction that previous monetary policy actions have initiated.

The monetary policy tool that is used on a regular basis is called open market operations. It is through open market operations that the Fed impacts the supply and demand for money, which in turn pushes short-term interest rates up or pulls them down.

The interest rate that the Fed influences is called the federal funds rate. This is the interest rate that banks charge each other for day-to-day borrowings.

When conducting open market operations, the Fed sets a target rate and then the FRB of New York buys or sells investment securities in order to either insert or remove money from the banking system. It works this way.

When the Fed wants to lower interest rates, they buy U.S. government bonds from financial institutions. When they want to raise interest rates, they sell U.S. government bonds to financial institutions. This impacts the supply and demand for money. It is through this mechanism that the federal funds rate is encouraged upward or downward.

Here is an illustration of how this works. Assume that you are a financial institution with which the Fed conducts open market operations. If the Fed is trying to increase economic activity, they will buy a bond from you. You will send the Fed your bond, and the Fed will give you cash—which you will deposit in your bank. Because the supply of money (deposits) has gone up and demand for money has not changed, interest rates will fall.

The impact on GDP occurs when banks lend the "new" money that was obtained through open market operations. When a bank lends the "new" money to a business or a consumer, the money that is borrowed is used to buy consumer goods or make investments. This increases both "C" and "I" in the GDP equation. The result is an increase in the GDP growth rate.

Think about it from a personal perspective. When interest rates go down, you are more likely to borrow money to buy a new car or a new television, to remodel your current home, or to build a new home. These types of transactions impact GDP in the areas of consumer spending (auto, TV, or remodeling) or investment (new home).

The opposite happens when the Fed wants to slow economic activity. Using the same personalized example where you are a bank, the Fed will sell you a bond and you will write a check from your account to pay for it. As a result, the money supply (deposit in the bank) goes down. And since there is now more demand for money than there is supply, interest rates go up.

When interest rates go up, you are less likely to borrow money to buy a car or a new television, to remodel your current home, or to build a new home. When you delay your purchases because the cost of borrowing is too high, GDP growth slows because of the reduced consumer spending (auto, TV, or remodeling) or investment (new home).

As indicated earlier, a troublesome current monetary policy issue is that the Fed has used most of its open market operations bullets. In December 2008, the federal funds rate was lowered to .25 percent. Yes, this is one quarter of one percent—effectively zero. The Fed can only reduce this rate to zero. Thus, there is not much ammunition left in the Fed's arsenal with which to encourage economic growth.

A complementary aspect of this policy dilemma is that consumers have become numb to interest rate changes. Instead of reacting to interest rates, they focus on the size of a loan payment. In recent years, banks have lengthened the life of auto loans and home mortgages. When the life of a loan is lengthened, the monthly loan payment goes down. Magically, consumers think they can now afford to buy more than would have been the case had the bank required a shorter loan life. Such loan life lengthening and related consumer thinking is a contributor to *Stupidomics*.

4

How an Economy Can Grow Forever

To illustrate the fostering of economic growth over time, economists use the production possibilities curve. This is shown in Figure 13. The production possibilities curve shows the trade-off between the production of one type of good and another. In other words, an economy has limited resources and can only produce so much of each type of good in order to meet marketplace demand.

When economists discuss growth possibilities, they look at the tradeoff between capital goods (goods that are used to make other goods) and consumer goods (goods that are used up in a relatively short time period). In order for an economy to grow, it must invest in capital goods, which are important for improving technology, improving operating processes, and improving education.

In Figure 13, the inner line represents the maximum amount of goods and services that can be produced each year with an existing level of capital goods (commonly called resources) in our hypothetical economy.

Figure 13
Production Possibilities Curve

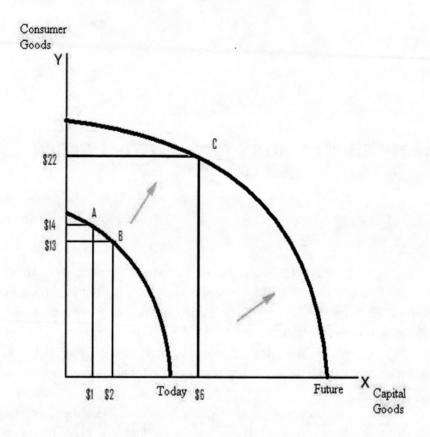

Using GDP as an example, and assuming no taxation or savings, at one extreme, this economy can produce $15 trillion of capital goods and no consumer goods. This is not an attractive economic position, for this society will perish since there will be no production of food and the other necessities of life.

At the other extreme, our hypothetical economy can produce $15 trillion consumer goods and no capital goods. In this case the economy will gradually grind to a halt. This is because all of the capital goods being used to make consumer goods will eventually wear out. Once worn out, there will be no capital goods with which to make anything. With no resources available to make consumer or capital goods, society will perish.

The key point is that in order to maintain consumer goods production at some level, society must produce some capital goods. To maintain the economic status quo, the amount of new capital goods produced must be equal to the amount of existing capital goods used up in the production of all goods.

Here is a more realistic example. Let's assume that our hypothetical economy is at a GDP sustaining level when producing $14 trillion consumer goods and $1 trillion capital goods. This is represented by point A in Figure 13. But the citizens of this hypothetical country are not happy with the standard of living. They want their children and grandchildren to have better goods and more of them. How can they accomplish this?

In order to provide more of everything in the future, the production possibilities curve must shift outward. When it does, more capital and consumer goods are available to society. Here is what must be done in order to shift the curve outward.

Parents today must give up some consumer goods in order to free up funds to make more capital goods. How much consumer spending must be given up depends on how much future growth is desired. For purposes of this illustration, let's assume that U.S. citizens decide to produce $2 trillion capital goods. To do so, society will need to give up an additional $1 trillion of consumer goods, which will lower total consumer goods to $13 trillion. This will move this society's production from point A on the Today's production possibilities curve to point B.

Note that total output at either point A or point B is $15 trillion, but output at point B is now allocated by society in a way that promotes growth.

Over time, as more capital goods are made and placed into productive use, the curve will shift outward as shown by the Future curve in Figure 13. Society at that future time might decide to operate a point "C" on this new curve. Once there, they will benefit from more consumer and capital goods. In our example, the future economy will produce $22 trillion of consumer goods and $6 trillion of capital goods, or a total of $28 trillion of total output.

One last point is appropriate. If society decides not to produce more capital goods by moving from point A to point B on today's curve, the economy will still grow. But the resulting future GDP will be significantly below the $26 trillion possible if more capital goods are produced.

This tradeoff illustrates the idea of opportunity cost, which is the cost of an alternative that is given up to do the alternative that is being done. The $1 trillion of consumer goods given up in order to produce $1 trillion more of capital goods is an opportunity cost to the present generation.

The trade-off is not exactly a one for one proposition as we have presented in our example. Rather, to produce an additional $1 trillion of capital goods, society must give up a little more than $1 trillion in consumer goods. This concept is more fully explained in the glossary.

The robust economy of the 1980s, 1990s, and early 2000s is, to some degree, a result of sacrifices made by our parents and grandparents. Here are two examples. In the 1950s, the Eisenhower administration used tax dollars to begin construction of the Interstate Highway system. The budget was balanced in most of those years.

This means that some consumer goods had to be foregone in order to divert funds to the Interstate system's construction. This system made travel faster and more efficient. The final result was that it stimulated economic growth and continues to provide benefits to the U.S. economy today.

The same is true of the space program. The Kennedy administration diverted tax dollars from consumer spending in order to fund space program expenditures. The research that was conducted in order to build rockets, communications equipment, and satellites was an investment in capital goods. Spinoffs from this research eventually found their way into the private sector. Entrepreneurs adapted space research into many of the products we take for granted today. A short list of the types of things that evolved from NASA research is presented in Table 3.

The important point is that, had the investments in highways and space technology not been made by our parents and grandparents at a cost of their personal consumption, we would not enjoy cell phones, satellite TV and radio, satellite weather forecasting, efficient highway travel, personal computers, and a whole host of other things that make life more enjoyable today.

The same concept applies to businesses when they invest in research and development. The money spent on research could be retained in the business. If this were done, profits would rise in the short run. Higher profits would allow more cash to be sent to stockholders in the form of dividends. But this would not be good for the long-term health of either the individual company or the U.S. economy. When a company retains cash and invests it in research and development, new products are spawned. These products contribute to improvements in productivity and societal well-being. This in turn adds to economic growth.

63

Table 3
NASA Spinoffs

Microcomputers	High-density Batteries
Breast cancer detection system	Satellite communications
Hang gliders	Programmable pacemaker
Scratch-resistant lenses	Solar energy
MRI	Dustbuster
Fire resistant clothing	Interactive computer training
Smoke detectors	Pollution control devices
Robotics	Doppler radar
Composite materials	Studless winter tires

Source: www.thespaceplace.com/nasa/spinoffs.html

In summary, the key to having more of everything in the future is to invest in capital goods today. The space program continues to be an attractive endeavor in this regard. As we go to press, momentum is building for an energy self-sufficiency initiative on a scale similar to that of 1960's space program. Such an effort will take time and will require sacrifice. The reward is that the production possibilities curve will eventually shift outward as a result of such a capital investment initiative and our economy will produce more of everything to the benefit of posterity.

5

The Rationale for Lowering Tax Rates

Some politicians argue that income tax rates should be lowered in order to stimulate economic growth. As we learned in our discussion of fiscal and monetary policy, it is appropriate to lower income tax rates in order to stimulate the economy. But, this is not always an advantageous fiscal policy action. Here's why.

The argument for lowering tax rates as a way to raise total tax revenue is drawn from a concept developed by Arthur Laffer who was a supply side economist in the Reagan Administration. His concept is usually illustrated through the use of a graph that is called a Laffer Curve. We present such a curve in Figure 14. This curve can be used to determine if an income tax rate reduction will result in an increase in total tax revenue or will lower such revenue. The impact on total tax revenue depends on where current income tax rates are in terms of the peak of the Laffer curve.

For sake of discussion, we assume that the top marginal U.S. tax rate is on the right side of the Laffer peak. This is illustrated at a 70 percent marginal tax rate on the Laffer curve. From this point, lowering the marginal tax rate to 50 percent will increase total tax revenue. If, on the other hand, the U.S. marginal tax rate is at 35 percent as shown in Figure 14, lowering the marginal income tax rate will result in a reduction in total tax revenue.

Economists do not agree on exactly where the peak of the Laffer curve is located. We use 50% for illustrative purposes only. Currently, the top U.S. marginal income tax rate is 35 percent. This means that a single taxpayer earning over $357,700 will pay tax of $.35 on each $1.00 of additional income earned above this level.

It is probable that the current marginal income tax rate of 35% is to the left of the Laffer curve peak, and if so, there is only one way to increase total tax revenue. This is to increase the top marginal tax rate above the current 35 percent level.

If the top marginal rate is lowered to 25 percent, then total tax revenue will fall. This in turn will increase the size of a budget deficit as well as the total national debt outstanding. Reducing the top marginal rate to increase tax revenue worked in the Reagan administration because marginal tax rates were to the right of the Laffer curve peak. The opposite impact was realized during the Clinton administration. When income tax rates were increased, total tax revenue went up and a budget surplus was generated.

Like all things that work once or twice to economic benefit, policymakers always "go to the well" once too often. The tax rate reduction well has run dry. To emphasize our last point, let's assume that the U.S. government reduces income tax rates to zero. This, if those who advocate for tax rate reductions in order to increase total tax revenue are correct, should result in infinite tax revenue flowing into the Treasury. Obviously that won't happen. A zero income tax rate will result in zero tax revenue.

Figure 14
Laffer Curve

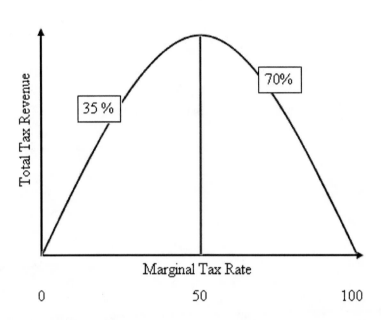

While reducing income tax rates to zero is an extreme example, it clearly shows the fallacy inherent in the argument that marginal tax rates should be lowered in order to raise total tax revenue. Because past administrations have lowered marginal income tax rates to a position that is now to the left side of the Laffer curve peak, future administrations will not be able to use tax rate cuts as a method of generating tax revenue from which to pay down the national debt.

We believe that those who seek to reduce income tax rates in order to increase tax revenue either don't understand the Laffer concept, are pursuing further tax cuts for selfish reasons, or are trying to buy votes. This is the type of thinking that promotes *Stupidomics*.

6

International Trade

In 1998, California based Coastcast Corporation was riding the crest of a golfing wave created by the Tiger Wood tsunami. For this manufacturer of titanium and stainless steel club heads, the possibilities seemed endless.

Notably, their customer list included the premier names in golf—Callaway, Titleist, Cobra, and Ping. In 1997, market share was climbing and sales hit a high of $150 million. However, by 2003 sales were down over 59 percent, almost 4,000 jobs were destroyed, and the company realized a net loss of over $10 million.

The reason? China! In just five years this irrepressible competitor captured a significant share of the worldwide golf club head market. Manufacturing jobs were lost in the U.S., shareholders' suffered financial distress, and employees needed to be trained for work in other career fields.

Foreign Made

China isn't the only source of imported goods. Indeed, foreign products are everywhere. We are golfers and don't normally pay attention to who manufactures the golfing products we use. However, as we developed this chapter, we conducted a little home-based research and discovered that our golf purchases are multi-national.

For example, out golf shoes, gloves, and towels were all made in China. We own golf shirts made in Honduras, Guatemala, Sri Lanka, Cambodia, India, and Pakistan. Our golf shorts came from Vietnam, the Philippines, and Mauritius. The golf umbrellas we carry were made in Thailand. Only the brand of golf ball we use is made in America.

Wage differentials are an aspect of the movement of manufacturing operations to developing countries. And this difference in wages is an important component in the application of a Macroeconomic 101 concept known as absolute and comparative advantage.

Absolute and Comparative Advantage

The idea behind absolute and comparative advantage is straight forward. Possessing an absolute advantage means that a nation can produce more of all types products than can its trading partners. Comparative advantage means one nation has the ability to produce more output from a given number of resource inputs than its trading partners are able to do. In other words, a comparative advantage accrues from an ability to produce something at lower cost than competitors.

To illustrate this concept, let's return to the example family we introduced in chapter two. For purposes of this example, we assume that the mother is the best accountant in the state and is also the best home cleaner. In economic terminology, she has an absolute advantage in both career areas.

Our mother can work as an accountant and earn $75,000 per year, or she can join a home cleaning firm and earn $35,000 per year--but she cannot do both. Thus, she must decide which alternative she will pursue. If she works as an accountant, her opportunity cost is the $35,000 of wages given up by not doing home cleaning. On the other hand, if she works as a home cleaner her opportunity cost of pursuing this career is the $75,000 in accounting earnings foregone.

Obviously, the mother has a comparative advantage in accounting skills and should choose to work as an accountant. Someone else in the community, who possesses a different set of opportunity costs for various skills, will perform the cleaning service.

The point of the above example is that comparative advantage is a relative concept. In a rational marketplace, participants evaluate the opportunity costs related to mutually exclusive choices and select the one with the lowest opportunity cost. This concept works the same way for nations.

The absolute/comparative advantage concept suggests that a nation should produce those goods for which it has a comparative advantage vis-à-vis another nation. A comparative advantage may accrue from favorable endowments of labor, land, or capital. By producing where it has a comparative advantage, each nation focuses its resources on its primary area of production superiority. The end result is that total global output is maximized. In the case of China, they have labor endowments that are favorable when compared to the US. Here's how it works.

Assume that the United States and China each have two workers. In the U.S., one worker can produce one dozen shorts per hour and the other can produce one dozen golf balls per hour. On the other hand, one Chinese worker can produce a dozen shorts per hour and another can produce one-half dozen golf balls per hour. The U.S. has an absolute advantage in golf balls but not in shorts as both firms produce at the same rate per hour.

In the U.S., the opportunity cost of producing two dozen shorts is one dozen of golf balls, and vice versa. In China, the opportunity cost of producing two dozen shorts is one-half dozen golf balls and the cost of producing one dozen golf balls is a dozen shorts. China has a comparative advantage related to the production of shorts since its opportunity cost is lower relative to that of the U.S. To maximize the total global output of these two items, China should produce all shorts and the U.S. should produce all golf balls. The two countries then trade shorts for golf balls.

As shown in Table 4, with specialization based on comparative advantage, total output per hour of shorts remains the same, whereas total output of golf balls increases by one-half dozen balls per hour. The only thing that has changed is who is making what based on each country's comparative advantage.

Our illustration assumes two products and two workers in order to simplify the explanation of this concept. Worldwide (WW), there are millions of products each with a differing comparative advantage from nation to nation. While the international trade discussion does not often use the absolute and comparative advantage terminology, this type of analysis is being made continually as nations seek to maximize production given limited quantities of scarce productive resources.

However the final production mix works out between nations, the key point is that by specializing in areas where there is a comparative advantage nations can expand worldwide output. They then trade with each other to achieve a maximum global benefit.

Table 4
Comparative Advantage Example

No Specialization or International Trade

| | United States | | China | | WW |
	Worker Hour	Dozen Output	Worker Hour	Dozen Output	Total Output
Shorts	1.0	**1.0**	1.0	**1.0**	**2.0**
Golf Balls	1.0	**1.0**	1.0	**.5**	**1.5**

With Specialization Based on Comparative Advantage and International Trade

| | United States | | China | | WW |
	Worker Hour	Dozen Output	Worker Hour	Dozen Output	Total Output
Shorts	----	----	2.0	**2.0**	**2.0**
Golf Balls	2.0	**2.0**	----	----	**2.0**

Nothing New

While jobs are being destroyed in the U.S. as a result of manufacturing moving overseas, this migration is not a new phenomenon. There is a long history of industries moving in order to take advantage of labor economies.

For example, in the middle part of the twentieth century, textile mills moved from New England to North Carolina and other southern states. Why? So they could lower labor costs. The southern states had a comparative advantage in labor. The recent movement of this industry to Mexico, China, and other developing countries is a continuation of this pattern.

Similarly, the U.S. automobile industry, as well as Japanese and other international firms opening plants in this country, have tended to locate in the south and southwest part of the country during the past 30 years. This occurred because southern states had a comparative advantage in labor costs compared to Michigan, Ohio, and Indiana.

For the US, a loss of jobs in the textile, automobile, and other industries means that research and development efforts must continue to focus on the discovery of new products that will drive the development of new industries, such as microcomputers did in the 1980's and 1990's and the Internet is doing in the twenty-first century. Many think that the next area of focus should be alternatives that substitute for oil based energy. We agree.

Until new jobs are created, there will be some economic pain. Those who are displaced by this movement will need to be retrained so they are ready to take advantage of higher paying jobs that will surely become available as the U.S. economy reinvigorates itself over the next several years.

Caution

It is our opinion that comparative advantage can be taken too far. To apply this concept effectively, the comparison of costs to produce should include not only the cash costs, but also the societal costs related to environmental protection, national health, and social welfare. All these requirements exist for the betterment of U.S. society, but exacerbate the comparative disadvantage related to production costs faced by U.S. firms.

For example, in the U.S. there are emission standards to protect the environment, safety standards to protect workers, and social requirements (for example the Americans with Disabilities Act) which add to the cost of manufacturing products and delivering services. These protections are not present to the same degree in China and other countries from which the U.S. imports products and services.

As a result, the U.S. economy continues to lose jobs that are outsourced to China, India, and other developing nations. For this and other reasons, foreign trade is not always conducted fairly for U.S. firms.

Second, there is a national defense consideration. Taken to the extreme, let's assume that all manufacturing is outsourced to other countries as a result of the comparative advantage concept. This would mean that U.S. GDP consists entirely of services. How then, do we defend ourselves? Who makes the tanks, airplanes, weapons, clothing, computer components, and other material we need to successfully prosecute a war?

Indeed, because of comparative advantage the U.S. has pretty much given up the manufacturing of steel, clothing, shoes, computers and computer chips, and a whole host of other consumer and business products.

Interestingly, discussions that center around international trade almost never mention national defense. We did not uncover any evidence that anyone in the U.S. government is monitoring foreign outsourcing from a national defense perspective. A primary reason we won WW II was our ability to produce the things that were needed in order to overwhelm our enemies. We are not confident that this competitive advantage still exists. We think this is an area where attention is warranted.

Stupidomics

7

Eliminating Stupidomics and Reducing the Risk of Economic Failure

To open our discussion of how to eliminate *Stupidomics*, a story about Casey Stengel breaking in a new left fielder seems appropriate. Casey was manager of the New York Yankees from 1949 to 1960. During his time with the Yankees he won seven World Series. He is in the baseball hall of fame and is considered one of the greatest managers of all time. He knew how to do things right.

As the story goes, Casey was breaking in a rookie left fielder in the latter part of his career. During a practice session, he was hitting balls to the rookie, and the rookie was having a hard time. He caught some, some went over his head, some dropped in front of him, and some rolled through his legs.

After a while, Casey became frustrated. He called the rookie in and said, "Give me your glove. I'll go to left field. You hit balls to me. I'll show you how it's done."

The rookie hit balls. Casey caught some, some went over his head, some dropped in front of him, and some rolled through his legs.

Getting more frustrated, Casey called the rookie over, put his arm around him and said, "Kid, you've got left field so messed up nobody can play it."

That's how Americans feel at the end of 2008. That the economy has been so messed up that no one knows how to fix it. While the economy is hurting, we believe that it can and will be fixed as we start to eliminate *Stupidomics*. Following are some suggestions that will help *Stamp Out Stupidomics*.

Education

As we stated in the introduction, it is unconscionable that we do not require our economic system to be taught in our public schools. How can Americans make good purchase decisions if they do not have a solid grounding in economics? How can Americans vote in an informed way if they do not understand the basics of fiscal and monetary policy? How, after experiencing the economic disaster of 2008 can the U.S. afford to continue to graduate students who are unschooled in economic understanding?

It is time to require that all high school students complete a course in economics in order to graduate. What is taught in the required course does not need to include all of the concepts that are included in economics textbooks. Such a course can omit topics like marginal productivity of labor; marginal propensity to consume and the multiplier effect; the money multiplier; and the technical distinction between demand and a change in demand, and supply and a change in supply, to name a few.

But, students should graduate from high school understanding Gross Domestic Product and how it is managed by the U.S. government and the Fed. Students should understand sacrifice and the role economics plays in allocating scarce resources among citizens. They should understand the idea of tradeoffs, and that sometimes, for the good of future generations we must give up some personal consumption today in order to invest in capital goods that will allow our children and grandchildren to have more of everything than we do.

These economic lessons should be more than theory. To be sure, theory is important, but application of theory is where success is achieved. Thus, teaching citizens how to use theory to achieve financial success and to vote intelligently are important lessons that should be imparted to every high school student in the United States.

To accomplish this, an economics course should include aspects of personal finance, often called applied economics. This course should provide instruction in cash management, checking and savings accounts, retirement accounts, sensible use of debt, investing, insurance management, and how to buy a home (including the need to save for a down payment).

Further, all borrowers who seek a home loan, and have credit card and automobile loan debt that amounts to more than 15 percent of disposable income, should be required to take a personal finance class. This class should require the preparation of a personal financial plan, including a budget, before a home loan can be made.

With consumers sending debt levels to all-time highs and bankruptcies running rampant, it is past time to educate Americans in economic fundamentals. Proper education will go a long way toward eliminating *Stupidomics,* which in turn will help the U.S. economy grow and prosper in a rational manner.

Financial Transparency

Education is a critical weapon in the campaign to eliminate *Stupidomics.* But education alone is not a cure all. Education must be supplemented with information that an educated citizenry can use in making choices between competing personal and political alternatives.

GDP growth rates, the budget deficit, inflation, interest rates, stock prices, and market movements are routinely reported in the popular press. These are important decision making tools.

In accounting, information must be useful to managers and investors in order to be valuable for decision making purposes. Accountants call this relevance.

To be relevant, information must contain three elements. First, it must be timely. In other words, information must be available when a decision needs to be made, not six months or a year after the time needed. Second, to be relevant information must be presented in a way that provides a basis for understanding past performance. And third, to be relevant information must be presented in a way that allows future earnings and cash flows to be understood and predicted.

For economic information to be relevant, it must be timely and must be presented in a way that shows where the economy has come from, where it is at, and where it is headed. This can be done by presenting key economic statistics in graphic form.

To illustrate how reporting of economic data might be improved, we use a portion of a press release from the Bureau of Economic Analysis ("BEA") dated September 26, 2008. The material released by the BEA is highlighted using italics. The graphic data was added by the authors in order to show how material might be more usefully presented in order to facilitate greater understanding of important debt management, employment, inflation, and GDP growth positions.

Bureau of Economic Analysis
National Economic Accounts
GROSS DOMESTIC PRODUCT:
　　　SECOND QUARTER 2008 (FINAL)
CORPORATE PROFITS:
　　　SECOND QUARTER 2008 (FINAL)

　　　Real gross domestic product -- the output of goods and services produced by labor and property located in the United States -- increased at an annual rate of 2.8 percent in the second quarter of 2008, (that is, from the first quarter to the second quarter), according to final estimates released by the Bureau of Economic Analysis. In the first quarter, real GDP increased 0.9 percent.

　　　The GDP estimates released today are based on more complete source data than were available for the preliminary estimates issued last month. In the preliminary estimates, the increase in real GDP was 3.3 percent (see "Revisions" on page 3).

　　　The increase in real GDP in the second quarter primarily reflected positive contributions from exports, personal consumption expenditures (PCE), nonresidential structures, federal government spending, and state and local government spending that were partly offset by negative contributions from private inventory investment, residential fixed investment, and equipment and software. Imports, which are a subtraction in the calculation of GDP, decreased.

　　　The acceleration in real GDP growth in the second quarter primarily reflected a larger decrease in imports than in the first quarter, an acceleration in exports, a smaller decrease in residential fixed investment, an acceleration in nonresidential structures, an upturn in state and local government spending, and an acceleration in PCE that were partly offset by larger decreases in inventory investment and in equipment and software.

We propose that the following, or something similar to it, be added in order to improve the decision usefulness of the information presented in the press release.

As a result of these changes, total consumer debt ended the second quarter at 98 percent of total GDP. The magnitude of this increase in consumer debt is shown in the following table.

Figure 15
Household Debt to GDP

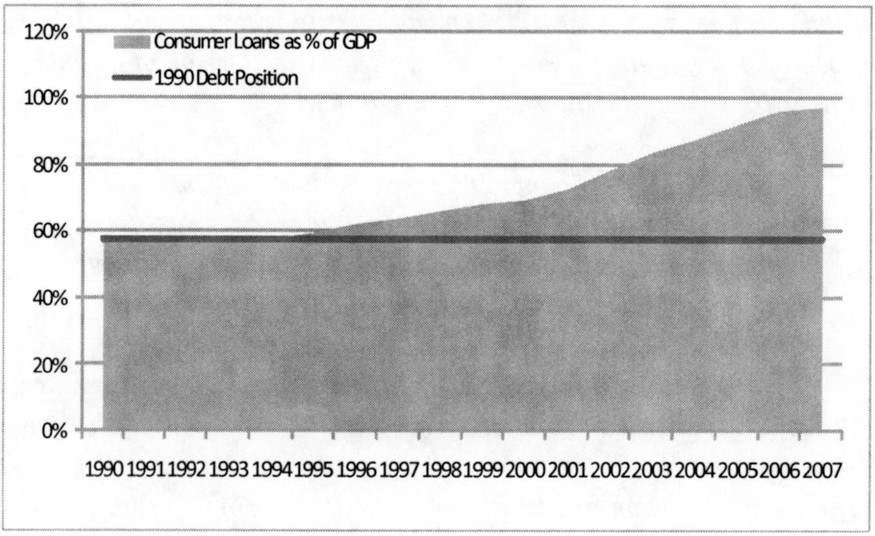

Source: Developed from Federal Reserve and Bureau of Economic Analysis data

Likewise, total government debt ended the quarter at 73 percent of GDP as shown in the following graph. This increase in total debt contributed to the decline in the value of the dollar against the euro and the yen.

Figure 16
Government Debt to GDP

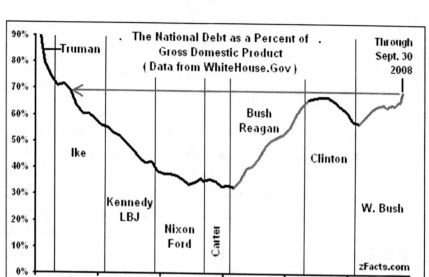

Source: http://zfacts.com/p/318.html. Adapted with permission.

These total debt positions are above historical norms, and the continued accumulation of debt by both households and the U.S. government were primary drivers of the reported GDP growth of 2.8 percent for the second quarter of 2008.

The data included in the BEA's press release is useful to economists and others who are trained in how to read and interpret this type of information. But, for the average American, the presentation is sterile and lacks historical perspective. As a result, the ability to predict how future movements in consumer and governmental debt levels will impact economic growth is not clearly presented. It lacks relevance.

The inclusion of the consumer and government debt graphs, with narrative, improves the presentation. From the graphs, a citizen can see that there is little room for additional borrowing by either consumers or the U.S. government.

Rather, those viewing these graphs might reasonably conclude that both consumers and the U.S. government must begin to reduce debt levels. When this happens, spending in "C" and "I" and "G" will slow down. As a result, GDP will be lower than would otherwise have been the case.

This is relevant information. This is useful information. This is transparent information. Too many graphs will diminish information usefulness, but the lack of graphs clearly does not help the average American who is seeking information on how the economy is performing and how monetary and fiscal policy actions are working. We think that the presentation of key U.S. economic success factors in graphic form will improve the ability of citizens to interpret economic data, which, in turn, will result in better economic decisions, which, in turn, will help eliminate *Stupidomics*.

Eliminate "Too Big To Fail" Thinking

In recognition of the negative impact of monopolies and cartels in restraint of trade, the Sherman Antitrust Act was passed in 1890. This act was passed because legislators understood that when corporations grow large enough to artificially inhibit or disrupt trade, the U.S. economy suffers. As a result, the Sherman Act made it illegal to conspire in restraint of both interstate and foreign trade. The Clayton Antitrust Act was passed in 1914 to expand the coverage of actions considered to be in restraint of trade.

The government used their powers under these Acts to break up AT&T in the early 1980s. The same powers were used to restrain Microsoft in the 1990s.

Today, as a result of the Sherman Act, monopolies are under regulatory control. However, the U.S. economy now faces danger from organizations that are considered too big to fail. This is as troublesome as was the case with unfettered monopolies. Here's why.

The "too big to fail" doctrine is most often employed in the financial institution industry. In 2008, institutions like Fannie Mae, Freddie Mac, and American International Group, to name a few were saved from failure by *The Economic Stabilization Act of 2008*. The rationale behind the bailout is that if these institutions are allowed to fail the U.S. economy will experience irreparable harm.

The "too big to fail" policy may actually promote failure. As these institutions grow larger and larger, they become more difficult to manage and control. Then, an over-egoed CEO "becomes smarter than everyone else" and begins to engage in high risk transactions in huge dollar amounts. While they are building their financial ponzi-like scheme, they take business from competitors that are following prudent management and financial practices. Of course, multi-million dollar salaries are paid to these "brilliant" executives as they are building their house of cards.

Then, when a bloated financial institution gets into difficulty, and they always do, the CEO looks to the federal government to bail them out. When the government does this, the bailout cost can be financed in one of two ways. Taxes can be raised to cover the bailout's cost, or the government can borrow the needed amount.

To our knowledge, the money to fund most bailouts has always been borrowed. This is dishonest and dishonorable. For borrowing to cover the cost of bailing out failing financial institutions is tantamount to a tax on the American public. The only problem is, the tax falls on future generations who are unrepresented in this process. Those who fought the American revolutionary war claimed that "taxation without representation is tyranny." Taxing future generations, yet unborn, is no less tyrannical.

The recently enacted $700 billion bailout package does three harmful things. First, it adds to an already too large governmental debt burden. Second, it reduces U.S. fiscal policy options for many years to come. Third, it once again confirms that those who manage these too-large-to-fail organizations are not superstars. They are just managers who rose to their Peter Principle. But they are dangerous because they know the government will not let their institutions fail. This mindset helps foster the next round of risky activity and ensuing bailout.

Enough!

To prevent this from happening again, the United States needs a Sherman-like act that breaks these institutions up before they get to a size where they can cause serious systemic economic harm. If there is a silver lining to the 2008 financial crisis cloud, it is that financial institutions are too important to the nation's economy to be left to the devices of those who manage them. They must be restrained to a size where allowing them to fail is a viable policy option. Further, as financial institutions grow larger and larger and are headed for too-big-to-fail status, they must be regulated to insure that the law is followed and prudent financial behavior exercised.

The banking industry has used a tool called the "HHI" which means the Herfindahl-Hirschman Index, a commonly accepted measure of market concentration. It is calculated by squaring the market share (dollar amount of deposits) for each bank in a market and then summing the resulting numbers. For a monopoly the HHI would be $100^2 = 10,000$. For a market consisting of five banks with shares of 25, 20, 20, 20, and 15 percent, the HHI is 2600 ($25^2 + 20^2 + 20^2 + 20^2 + 15^2 = 2050$). The HHI increases both as the number of banks in the market decreases and as the difference in size between those banks increases. When banks propose mergers they may be required to sell off one or two of the branches before getting approval if the new HHI is in excess of 1800 points and if it represents more than a 200 point increase. Part of the fix for the "too-big-to-fail" problem may be to determine a market share on a national level that is too concentrated, that is too big to fail, and not allow any bank to grow beyond that size.

Further, the Glass-Steagall Act should be reinstituted in modernized form. Our grandparents put a wall between banking, insurance, investment banking, and real estate firms for a reason. The reason is that, when combined into one large organization they cannot be managed prudently. The financial crisis of 2008 highlighted the mischief that can be visited upon the U.S. economy when institutions are allowed to compete and conspire in all of these related industries at the same time.

Finally, higher capital requirements are a must as financial institutions grow larger and larger. The idea behind this suggestion is that as a financial institution grows in size it becomes riskier, and as it grows riskier it becomes a potential burden on the U.S. economy. This, as we have recently seen, is unacceptable. The economy must be protected by requiring that rapidly growing organizations increase capital levels above traditional growth rate levels.

For example, a financial institution with $500 billion in assets might need a seven percent capital to asset ratio, whereas a financial institution with $1 trillion in assets might need a 10 percent capital ratio. Further, a $500 billion financial institution growing at a 15 percent annual rate might need capital of 10 percent, whereas an institution of the same size growing at a 5 percent annual rate might need only a seven percent capital ratio.

Research should be conducted in this area to determine at what size and growth rate capital requirements need to be increased. Ratcheting up capital requirements will serve as a growth deterrent and will provide an additional margin of safety as a financial institution's risk increases as it grows.

Regulatory Considerations

Banking products are commodity-like and one banker doesn't have any significant intellectual or creative advantage over the next one. A checking account is a checking account and a savings account is a savings account. Likewise, a mortgage loan is a mortgage loan and an automobile loan is an automobile loan. There is really no way for one banker to make his or her product more attractive than that of the banker across the street—unless they take on greater risk.

Thus, since banking products do not really differ from one institution to the next, under normal economic conditions banks should not be able to grow too fast. Indeed, it is hard for a bank to grow at much more than the rate of inflation. This is because bank growth is generated primarily from the interest paid on deposits and from deposits that can be lured away from competitors.

Exceptions to this inflation based growth idea are banks that operate in areas experiencing rapid economic growth. This is because, as people move from Michigan to Florida, they bring their deposits with them. This transfer of deposits does two things. It lowers the growth rate of Michigan banks and increases the growth rate of Florida banks--but only during the period of time during which the migration from Michigan to Florida is being experienced.

Because of this, it seems reasonable to apply additional regulatory scrutiny to banks that grow at more than twice the rate of inflation. CAMEL ratings of financial institutions should be disclosed. A CAMEL rating is developed by bank regulators when they conduct an examination. CAMEL is an acronym for Capital adequacy, Asset quality, Management capacity, Earnings quality, and Liquidity position. Regulators are reluctant to disclose this assessment. However, regulators are the ones best able to determine the quality of a banking operation and the risk inherent in both its balance sheet structure and its earnings generation model. Disclosing the CAMEL rating will increase transparency and subject banking organizations to the discipline of the marketplace.

In addition, if a firm is rescued with public money, it should lose the right to managerial independence following such a bailout. Among other things, this should include appointment of all members of the board of directors by an independent qualifying body. Those that qualify for board membership should be required to hold a professional license in a financial area, such as Certified Public Accountant or Charter Financial Analyst.

Professional directors will add financial savvy to a board of directors and eliminate the cronyism that results when the CEO decides who should serve on his or her board. Management often short-changes director fees because they feel that directors do not add value to a firm's business proposition. We do not agree. Directors are supposed to be watchdogs who act on behalf of shareholders to insure that management acts in the best interest of owners and society. They should be paid a director's fee that is large enough to insure they do their job independently and professionally.

To qualify independent board members, an NCAA clearinghouse-like body should be employed. This group would authenticate the credentials of those willing to serve in a directorship capacity. A board of directors for a bailed-out firm would be selected from this pool on a random basis.

Further, senior officers of any institution that is bailed out with public money should be fired and banned from working in that industry as an employee or consultant. This should be a lifetime ban.

Financial penalties should be assessed on those who manage a financial institution to failure. Such penalties should include forfeiture of any existing severance agreement and any contingent compensation agreements. This should be built into any contract that an institution enters into with senior and executive managers.

Finally, bonuses and other types of performance based compensation awarded to senior and executive managers should have a deferral provision. This provision would accrue earned compensation, but it would not be paid for at least five years, and then, amounts deferred would only be paid if the organization's performance remains above the industry average as shown in the five year cumulative total return graph included in the Definitive 14A Proxy Statement filed with the SEC.

8

Sacrifice and Changing Expectations

Sacrifice is NOT a dirty word. In fact, it is sacrifice that underlies economic thinking. A commonly used definition of economics is: *Economics is the study of how people in society make choices in order to satisfy their wants.* When consumers make choices, they must often sacrifice one thing to gain another.

People in society have an unlimited shopping basket full of wants. But, given scarce resources, people cannot have everything they want. Thus, person by person and household by household, decisions must be made as to what will be purchased with limited resources. These decisions are embodied in questions such as: What will I buy with my available income? How will I spend my time?

Economic decisions must be made because there are too many people and not enough resources to provide everyone with everything they want. For example, every household in America might like a home on the beach. Or every household might like to earn a $1 million annual income. While these wants are worthy, they are not economic realities. The U.S. economy doesn't have enough resources to provide everything to everyone.

Thus, most of us have to settle for what we are able earn based on our talent, training, and experience. And, we must decide where to live and what to buy based on our earned income. This means that we must make choices, and choices among competing alternatives mean that we must sacrifice one thing to gain another. Sometimes this is painful.

But sacrifice is not a bad thing. Indeed, when we have to work hard to gain something, we appreciate what we gain much more than if it was simply given to us. Intuitively, most Americans know this. The trouble is that we periodically forget this truism. In recent years, we seem to have collectively forgotten how to live with constraint. We want a thing now and we are willing to go into debt to get it.

This way of thinking starts slowly, but then herd mentality takes over, and before we know it too many people are following one another into financial difficulty. That happened in the 1920s and led to the Great Depression. It led to the rampant inflation of the 1970s, the stock market bubble of the 1990s, and the housing bubble of the 2000s.

Eventually, as our grandmother's used to say, people need to be "brought down a peg or two." In other words, someone must lead society out of these psychological crazes. Otherwise, some event will jolt society out of it. Unfortunately, in recent times leadership has been lacking and it has taken a jolt to get the attention of those who seek to lead the country.

Following is an example of how leadership worked to the benefit of the U.S. economy. In the 1970s, inflation was running at double digit levels and the U.S. economy experienced an extended recession which lasted from 1973 to 1975. Unemployment averaged seven percent from 1975 to 1980 while inflation averaged 7.8 percent over this same period. In fact, in 1979 the unemployment rate ended the year at 6 percent and the annualized inflation rate stood at 13.2 percent. Economists refer to this as stagflation. Ronald Reagan added the unemployment rate to the inflation rate and called it the misery index.

It was in this high unemployment, high inflation environment that President Carter appointed Paul Volcker as Chairman of the Federal Reserve Board in August 1979. Recognizing that inflation was eroding the purchasing power of the dollar, and that an inflation psychology had visited agony upon consumers and businesses, Volcker changed the focus of the Fed's monetary policy actions.

Rather than targeting interest rate levels, Volcker adopted a policy of controlling the growth rate of the money supply. The money supply is defined as the total amount of money available in an economy at a particular point in time. Economists define money at several levels, depending on how easily it can be managed. In this classification scheme, money that can be managed the easiest is called M1, and consists primarily of cash and checking accounts. Similarly, M2 consists of M1 plus savings and money market checking accounts.

In an earlier chapter, we discussed how the Fed conducts open market operations. It is primarily M1 that is impacted as the Fed buys and sells securities to influence interest rates movements. Prior to 1979, the Fed used open market open market operations to move interest rates up or down. During this time, the Fed's policy of targeting interest rates allowed the money supply to grow rapidly. Monetarists believe that inflation tends to move in concert with money supply growth, and this was clearly the case in the 1970's.

During his tenure as Chairman, Volcker restricted the money supply growth rate to a range of two to four percent. His actions reduced the growth rate of the money supply (deposits) while the demand for money (loans) continued to increase rapidly. The result was that interest rates went up.

Interest rates not only went up, they skyrocketed. Between 1980 and 1982, the federal funds rate, a primary short-term interest rate, moved from 10 percent in January 1979 to 17.6 percent in April 1980, back down to 9 percent by July 1980, and reached its peak of 19.1 percent in July 1981.

Looking back, this was inflation's high water mark. From its peak of 13.5 percent in 1981, it fell to three percent by 1984. Volcker's focus on management of the money supply worked, but not without economic pain. The U.S. economy suffered a severe recession that lasted from 1980 to 1982. But, once inflation was subdued, the U.S. economy started a prolonged period of low inflation with sustained economic growth.

Very few Americans know his name, but most households in the U.S. have benefitted from his leadership. We consider Paul Volcker an American hero.

9

Final Word

We have attempted to present the essence of the U.S. economy in a meaningful way. Our intent is to present macroeconomics in a manner that readers find instructive. By doing so, it is our hope that we have whetted your appetite to learn more about how our economic system works.

More importantly, we hope that you will support efforts to teach our economic system in our public schools. Some say that knowledge is power, and knowledge is certainly important in this regard. But the ability to apply knowledge to our personal and national best interest is even more important. This can only be accomplished through an educated citizenry. And that is the thought that spawned this book.

Readers might conclude from our recommendations that we are liberal in our approach to economic thinking. Reality is actually the opposite. We are fiscal conservatives. We believe that the U.S. budget should be balanced except in extreme circumstances. And once that circumstance is ended, any debt incurred to resolve it should be repaid and the U.S. budget brought back into balance.

We also believe in free markets. However, when institutions are badly and unethically managed and need help from the U.S. government in order to sustain themselves, such help represents a hidden tax on American citizens. In these cases, those who are responsible for this hidden tax should be held accountable in a meaningful and remedial way.

Finally, we don't want to seem overly pessimistic, but we think Americans should be aware of how deep of a hole has been dug over the past quarter century through the employment of *Stupidomics*. That hole is deep, as total national debt at the end of 2008 is approaching 85 percent of GDP and total consumer debt is at about 100 percent of GDP.

It is time to follow the rule of holes, which says: Once you find yourself in a hole, stop digging.

In order to return total national debt to the 1980 level of 40 percent of GDP, the U.S. economy will have to grow to about $28 trillion from its present level of $13 trillion. If GDP grows by five percent per year, and no further debt is added to the present total of $11 trillion, it will take 16 years to accomplish this task. That means that we must stop digging the debt hole until 2025. Of course, if we keep adding to the national debt burden, it will take even longer.

We believe that, if the nature of an economic problem is presented in an honest and understandable manner, Americans will follow prudent economic leadership in an effort to eliminate that problem. Such leadership is needed in order to *Stamp Out Stupidomics* from the American economy.

Glossary and Amplifications

This section presents definitions of terms used throughout the book. This is done to aid reader understanding of selected economic concepts. In some cases, we amplify a previous discussion by adding underlying assumptions related to a concept, or additional information is presented that adds insight into a concept in a more academic manner.

Absolute Advantage. The ability of a nation to produce a product or to deliver a service at a lower cost per unit than competitors. Unit costs are normally labor and resource.

Circular Flow Concept. The circular flow concept assumes that the seller receives the identical amount that the buyer spends, and that goods and services flow in one direction and money flows in the opposite direction. Other simplifying assumptions in the final circular flow diagram presented in this book are:

1. All the income that is earned by households from the factors of production (land, labor, capital, and entrepreneurship) is spent, taxed away, or saved by business, whether nationally or through foreign trade.

2. Normal leakages from the most simple of the models shown in Figure 2, are taxation, saving, and imports and exports. These leakages are eliminated step by step as we move from the most basic model in Figure 2 to the five-sector model shown in Figure 8.
3. This model also is a representation of Say's Law: Supply creates its own demand. Thus whatever produced will be purchased by households.
4. The multiplier effect related to saving is not illustrated in our circular flow discussion, but is explained in this section (see Multiplier Effect).

Comparative Advantage. The ability to produce a product or to deliver a service at a lower relative cost than other producers are able to meet, whether the other producer is a person, a firm, or another nation.

Gross Domestic Product ("GDP"). GDP is the total market value of all goods and services produced by the factors of production located within a nation's borders. The development of GDP was presented in the discussion of the circular flow where the GDP = C + I + G + X formula was developed. To be considered in GDP, the key definitional term is "goods and services produced." Items for which dollars are exchanged but the market value of the transaction is NOT included in GDP include:

1. **Securities Trading.** The market value of stocks, bonds, and other securities traded in the marketplace. Here's how it works. If a security sells for $1,000, and there is a fee of $50 for brokerage commissions, only the $50 is included in GDP.
2. **Government Transfer Payments.** These are payments for which no productive service is rendered in exchange for the payment. Examples are Social Security benefits, veteran benefits, and unemployment insurance payments.

Since nothing is produced, the payments are not included in GDP.

3. **Private Exchanges.** These can include gifts from a parent to a child or similar types included. Examples here are garage sales, flea markets, and sales of used items on Ebay. The value of the item sold in this way was included in GDP in the year the item was manufactured. Thus, assets that are resold do not meet the GDP definition.

4. **House and Handy-man Work.** When one parent stays at home to clean, care for children, and do general home maintenance, the value of these items is not included in GDP. The services have value to the family performing them, but they are not included in GDP since there is no free market exchange.

5. **The Shadow Economy.** This has two components. One is illegal activity, such as the sale of illegal drugs, illegal gambling, and illegal prostitution. The second is the cash based economy where exchanges are legal but payments are only made in cash. Because of this, they not reported and taxed. Examples include payments for babysitting and snow shoveling to teenagers, or small businesses that only report 70 to 80 percent of total revenue. Estimates of the value of the shadow economy transactions in the U.S. range from $3 to $4 trillion, which understates GDP by 20 to 30 percent. Indeed, if taxes were paid on average shadow economy transactions of $3.5 trillion, assuming a 15% average federal income tax rate, tax revenue would amount to $525 billion. This is enough to eliminate the current U.S. budget deficit.

Inflation. A sustained increase in prices in an economy. In the U.S., the most commonly used measure of inflation is the Consumer Price Index. This index is developed by the Bureau of Labor Statistics ("BLS") using a market basket of goods and services that a "typical" consumer would consume over the course of a year. Data is collected primarily in urban areas. The BLS indicates that data on prices is retrieved from about 23,000 businesses and about 50,000 landlords. The CPI is developed using sampling techniques and may not relate to the specific purchase patterns of individual households.

Money Multiplier. In the U.S., a fractional reserve banking system is employed. This means that for every dollar that banks have on deposit, they must maintain some percentage of total deposits on reserve with the Fed. At the current time, the average reserve requirement on all types of bank depositions is about 10 percent. Thus, banks may loan or invest $.90 of every $1.00 on deposit.

The formula for calculating the deposit expansion effect (multiplier) is: Deposit Expansion Multiplier = 1/Required Reserve Percent, or (in our example) 1/.10 = 10. This means that each new dollar of deposits injected into the banking system will, with no leakages, become $10. It works this way.

When the Fed conducts monetary policy, the Fed buys or sells securities to financial institutions. This infusion of funds eventually becomes deposits. For purposes of illustration, assume that bank A receives $1 million in new reserves. They keep reserves of $100 thousand and lend $900 which becomes deposits in other banks. The other banks, keep reserves of $90 thousand ($90 x 10%) and lends the remaining $810 thousand. These loans amounts are deposited in other banks and become lendable funds. This process continues until the initial infusion of $1 million becomes $10 million in the U.S. banking system.

Obviously, when the Fed infuses new deposits in the banking system, interest rates fall and more households borrow money to buy goods and services. This causes GDP to grow. The opposite happens when the Fed wants to slow the economy down. They withdraw deposits from the banking system and this causes interest rates to rise, fewer loans to be made, and the deposit base in the banking system to shrink. In this case, if the Fed withdraws $1 million in deposits, the ultimate result on total deposits in the banking system will be shrinkage of $10 million.

The previous discussion was simplified in order to illustrate how actions by the Fed impact GDP growth. As with other economic models, there are simplifying assumptions. These are:

1. The total amount loaned by one bank is not always deposited in another bank.
   a. First, some of the amount loaned my be held in cash.
   b. Second, banks do not loan 100 percent of their reserves. They may hold excess reserves for liquidity purposes.
   c. Third, they may use some of the funds to purchase buildings and equipment.

Economists estimate that the M1 (mostly checkable deposits and cash) deposit multiplier ranges from 2.5x to 3.0x of the deposit base (cash and amounts held with the Fed) in the U.S. banking system.

Peter Principle. In a system, every person will rise to a level or responsibility where he/she is incompetent to perform the duties of the position to which he/she has been elevated.

Production Possibilities Curve. A curve that shows all possible combinations of GDP that can be produced in one year assuming that:

1. All resources are fully and efficiently employed.
2. Factors of production (land, labor, and capital) cannot be changed during the year.
3. Technology (including the level of education) does not change during the year.

Obviously all of these factors are changing during any given year. However, economists make these simplifying assumptions in order to illustrate the concept. As a practical matter, the changes that occur in any one year are not significant enough to invalidate the concept that the production possibilities curve illustrates. Indeed, by sacrificing some consumer goods in the near-term by producing more capital goods and investing in education, we are trying to improve our societal position in a way that allows more of everything to be produced in the long-term. When this happens, more people have jobs, income levels rise, and society is better off than if they had not sacrificed in this manner.

In our text discussion, we have assumed that the production possibilities curve is a straight line. When the line is curved, as we show it Figure 13, the opportunity cost of giving up one thing to gain another increases by more than a one-for-one tradeoff. In other words, in order to gain an additional $1 trillion of capital goods, a society might have to give up $1.5 trillion in consumer good, rather than the $1 trillion we used in our example.

Spending Multiplier. The multiplier effect is associated with the circular flow and aggregate demand. Specifically, it can be used to estimate how much GDP will expand when there is a change in spending patterns by government, business, or consumers. Economists call this a change in autonomous spending. The impact on GDP is based on the portion of income that consumers spend and save. For example, assume that consumers spend 80 percent of their income and save 20 percent.

In economics, the 80 percent is called marginal propensity to consume ("MPC") and the 20 percent is called marginal propensity to save ("MPS"). The multiplier is calculated by dividing the MPS into one. In this example, one divided by .20 equals five. This means that if autonomous spending increases by $100 million, then GDP will increase by $500 million.

How does this happen? When new money (autonomous spending) is injected into the circular flow, it will circulate over and over until the final impact on GDP is realized. For example, when government borrows to increase spending, this is an increase in autonomous spending. The amount that is borrowed, say $100 million, when it flows through households during the second round. When households receive the $100 they will spend $80 and save $20. This will continue until the full $500 million increase in GDP is realized.

In the United States, the multiplier is estimated at 1.9 times for changes in autonomous spending. A similar multiplier impact can be achieved with tax cuts. Here, the impact is 1.2 times the tax reduction.

It should be noted that the multiplier can work in reverse. If autonomous spending is reduced or taxes are increased, GDP will fall by the same 1.9 times or 1.2 times, respectively.

A full discussion of this concept is beyond the scope of this book. Those who are interested in the full scope of the multiplier should review a macroeconomics textbook.

Unemployment. This measure represents the number of working age Americans who are not working but are willing to work, able to work, and are actively seeking work. The unemployment statistic is developed by the BLS by surveying 60,000 households on a monthly basis. This survey is used to determine unemployment in four different classifications.

1. Frictional. This type of unemployment occurs when a person leaves a job, is laid-off, or simply quits. While between jobs, their employment is temporary and they are expected to find new jobs.
2. Cyclical. This type of unemployment relates to recessions. Those that lose their job as a result of an economic downturn associated with a normal economic cycle are classified here.
3. Seasonal. This type of unemployment relates to industries that only operate at certain times of the year. Workers who are out of a job when a business is out of

season are classified here. For example, farm workers and ski area workers.

4. Structural. This type of unemployment relates to a change in societal preferences or is caused by competition. For example, the loss of jobs in the U.S. when manufacturing is outsourced to China is structural. The jobs are gone, will not be coming back, and workers need to be retained so that they can qualify for jobs in different career areas.

Test of Economic Understanding

Macroeconomics

Name _____

Multiple Choice - - 4 Points Each
Choose the best, or most complete answer.

1.   Economics is the study of how society:

   A. Makes choices among competing alternatives
   B. Satisfies consumer wants
   C. Allocates scarce materials
   D. All of the above

2.   The space program should be reduced in size and the money
        saved should be spent on funding education. This statement
        is:

   A. An example of normative economics
   B. An example of positive economics
   C. Just common sense
   D. None of the above

3.   When we measure the cost of anything by what has to be
        given up in order to have it, we call the thing that is given
        up:

   A. A difficult decision
   B. A comparative loss
   C. An absolute cost
   D. An opportunity cost

4. If the price of a Chevy Cobolt is raised from $19,000 to $20,000, then, all other things constant, the market should experience:

    A. An increase in demand
    B. Stay the same
    C. A decrease in demand
    D. A decrease in the quantity demand

5. Which of the following is NOT one of the three major economic questions a society must answer:

    A. What will be produced
    B. How the government will regulate it
    C. For whom will it be produced
    D. How will it be produced

6. If an economy experiences an increase in population, then, according to the laws of supply and demand, there should be:

    A. An increase in demand for goods and services
    B. A shortage of oil
    C. A need to expand the role of government
    D. Both A and C

7. Which of the following is not an economic goal of government?

    A. Promoting high and sustained economic growth
    B. Maintaining stable prices
    C. Maintaining low unemployment
    D. Providing public goods

8.   Inflation is?

A. Good for the economy
B. An international event
C. A sustained increase in the price level
D. Something the FRB likes

9.   The definition of gross domestic product includes:

A. Production within the nation's borders within one year
B. The market value of annual final product
C. Production in the shadow economy
D. Both A and B are included in the definition

10.   Which of the following is not a measure of inflation?

A. Consumer Price Index
B. Gross Domestic Product Deflator
C. Consumer Confidence Index
D. None of the above

11.   Unemployment has a cost to society. That cost can best be defined in economic terms as:

A. Loss of profit incentive
B. Loss of GDP output
C. The law of increasing costs
D. Both A and B

12.   If we spend 90 percent of an increase in our real disposable income, economists call this:

A. Marginal propensity to consume
B. Helping the economy grow
C. Consumer confidence
D. A good year

13.   In economic terms, saving is defined as:

A. Dollars saved by controlling costs
B. Real disposable income minus consumption
C. Individual actions aimed at controlling costs
D. What someone else does
E. A real good idea

14.   Which of the following is not part of the business cycle?

A. Trough
B. Peak
C. Government fiscal policy
D. Expansion
E. Recession

15.   The tools of fiscal policy are:

A. Electoral College
B. The Federal Reserve
C. Taxing and Spending
D. Budget Deficits

16. The tools of monetary policy:

    A. Printing coin and currency
    B. The discount rate, open market operations, and reserve requirements
    C. Printing money and getting it into consumers hand
    D. Money velocity, monetary growth, and inflation

17. The Federal Reserve System is:

    A. Is the Central Bank of the United States
    B. Managed by the Treasury Department
    C. Reports to the President
    D. An arm of the U.S. Senate

18. An economy is experiencing low rates of unemployment with high inflation. An appropriate policy action following a Keynesian strategy might be to:

    A. Increase taxes and/or decrease government spending
    B. Decrease taxes and/or increase government spending
    C. Decrease taxes and/or decrease government spending
    D. Increase taxes and/or decrease government spending

19. The money supply in the United States is controlled by:

    A. Congress (in particular, the Senate Committee on Banking and Finance)
    B. The commercial banking industry
    C. The U.S. Treasury Department
    D. The Federal Reserve Board
    E. The New York Stock Exchange

20.   If a nation's depreciation exceeds its gross investment, we can say that:

A. Net investment is positive
B. Net investment is zero
C. The nation's stock of capital is growing
D. The nation's stock of capital is declining
E. The nation's GDP will rise

21.   Fiscal policy refers to the use of:

A. Interest rates by the Federal Reserve System
B. Business policies to increase competition
C. The government budget to impact taxation and spending
D. The growth of the money supply

22.   Which of these events would likely reduce consumer spending?

A. An increase in personal income tax rates
B. A general decrease in interest rates
C. A decrease in stock prices
D. A reduction in the rate of unemployment

23.   The discount rate is the interest rate at which:

A. The Federal Reserve lends to commercial banks
B. Commercial banks lend to each other
C. The public lends to the federal government
D. The Federal Reserve lends to the U.S. Treasury
E. Commercial banks lend to the public

24.   If the rate of growth in an economy is 3 percent, inflation is 4 percent, and the nominal rate of interest is 8 percent, what is the real rate of interest?

A. 4 percent
B. 5 percent
C. 6 percent
D. 7 percent
E. 8 percent

25.   The current chairman of the FRB is:

A. Paul Volcker
B. Alan Greenspan
C. Ben Bernanke
D. T. Boone Pickens
E. Henry Paulson

For answers to the Test of Economic Understanding please visit www.stupidomics.com.

LaVergne, TN USA
12 January 2010
169703LV00004B/4/P